The US Air Force After Vietnam

Postwar Challenges and Potential for Responses

by

DONALD J. MROZEK
Senior Research Fellow
Airpower Research Institute

Air University Press
Maxwell Air Force Base, Alabama 36112-5532

December 1988

Library of Congress Cataloging-in-Publication Data

Mrozek, Donald J.
 The US Air Force after Vietnam: postwar challenges and potential for responses / by Donald J. Mrozek.
 p. cm.
 Bibliography: p.
 Includes Index.
 1. United States—Military policy. 2. Vietnamese Conflict, 1961-1975—Public opinion. 3. Public opinion—United States. 4. United States. Air Force. I Title. II. Title: United States Air Force after Vietnam.
 UA23.M76 1988   88-7476
 355'.0335'73—dc 19   CIP

ISBN 1-58566-024-8

First Printing December 1988
Second Printing July 2001
Third Printing April 2004

Disclaimer

This publication was produced in the Department of Defense school environment in the interest of academic freedom and the advancement of national defense-related concepts. The views expressed in this publication are those of the authors and do not reflect the official policy or position of the department of Defense or the United States government.

This publication has been reviewed by security and policy review authorities and is cleared for public release.

Air University Press
131 West Shumacher Avenue
Maxwell AFB AL 36112-6615
http://aupress.maxwell.af.mil

To

Dianne and Joseph

CONTENTS

Chapter		Page
	DISCLAIMER	ii
	FOREWORD	vii
	ABOUT THE AUTHOR	ix
	PREFACE	xi
	ACKNOWLEDGMENTS	xiii
1	**Introduction: The Scope of the Study**	1
	Notes	4
2	**Vietnam in History**	5
	The Continuing Relevance of the Vietnam Era	7
	The Emergence of History and Advocacy	10
	Vantage Points and Visions	15
	Principles or Preferences	18
	Historical Reflections and a Grasp at the Future	22
	Notes	30
3	**Interpreting Vietnam: School Solutions**	37
	Learning at Leavenworth	37
	Spreading the Word	43
	Training and Learning	45
	Notes	49
4	**Post-Vietnam Events and Public Discourse**	53
	National Security Issues and the Post-Vietnam Press	54
	Leaders and Their Memories	58
	Vietnam in Public Memory	62

Chapter		Page
	Thought and Feelings	65
	Notes	66
5	**The Congress and National Security after Vietnam: Business as Usual?**	69
	The Cold War Consensus and the Issue of "Normalcy"	69
	Surveying Congressional Views, 1984	71
	Common Ground	73
	The Distinctiveness of Proadministration Viewpoints	81
	Sources of Skepticism	86
	Congress and the Military: Politics, Threat, and "Normalcy"	89
	Notes	90
6	**Alternative Visions: The World beyond Vietnam**	95
	Other Wars, Other Analogies	95
	Beyond Crisis	98
	Beyond Deterrence	104
	Masters of Our Fate	108
	Notes	109
	APPENDIX A	115
	APPENDIX B	119
	INDEX	123

FOREWORD

In this study, Dr Donald J. Mrozek probes various groups of Americans as they come to grips with the consequences of the Vietnam War. He poses far more questions than he answers, and some of what he says may invite strong dissent. Yet it will serve its author's purpose if something here provokes creative thinking and critical reexamination, even of some long-cherished ideas. Viewing the Vietnam War as a logical outcome of American defense thinking has challenging implications, as does seeing the "cold war consensus" on foreign affairs as an oddity.

Yet this is not a litany of objection and protest. For example, Doctor Mrozek raises serious questions about how the contemporary notion of deterrence has emerged; and dealing with such questions forthrightly could make deterrence more effective. So, too, questioning the past relationship of military professionals with the mass media is not an assignment of guilt but an invitation to develop a beneficial and cooperative relationship. Nor is this study a tale of gloom and despair; it is rather an appeal for self-consciousness and self-awareness. It is a plea for us to take command of the problems that beset us by taking control of ourselves first.

SIDNEY J. WISE
Colonel, USAF
Commander
Center for Aerospace Doctrine,
Research, and Education

ABOUT THE AUTHOR

Dr Donald J. Mrozek

Donald J. Mrozek is professor of history at Kansas State University, where he has taught since 1972. He earned both his MA and PhD degrees at Rutgers University, and his dissertation study on defense policy during the presidency of Harry Truman yielded articles in publications such as *Military Affairs* and the *Business History Review*. Later research in wartime and postwar defense issues resulted in articles in such journals as *Annals of Iowa* and *Missouri Historical Review*. In 1980 his article "The *Croatan* Incident: The US Navy and the Problem of Racial Discrimination after World War II" appeared in *Military Affairs*. Also in 1980 he coedited *The Martin Marauder and the Franklin Allens: A Wartime Love Story* with Robin Higham and Jeanne Louise Allen Newell. With his colleague Robin Higham, he coedited *A Guide to the Sources of US Military History*, including the 1981 and 1986 supplementary volumes.

Doctor Mrozek has also researched, published, and taught in the area of American culture. Some of his publications have fused the areas of military and cultural history. His essay "The Cult and Ritual of Toughness in Cold War America" appeared in *Rituals and Ceremonies in Popular Culture*, ed. Ray Browne, in 1980. In 1984 "The Interplay of Metaphor and Practice in the US Defense Department's Use of Sport" was published in the *Journal of American Culture*. In 1985 "Sport and the American Military: Diversion and Duty" appeared in the centennial issue of the *Research Quarterly for Exercise and Sport.*

One of his more recent sole-authored military history publications, titled "The Limits of Innovation: Aspects of Air Power in Vietnam," appeared in the January–February 1985 issue of *Air University Review.* In 1986 *Air University Review* also published his essay "In Search of the Unicorn," a discussion of the broad development of military reform movements since the Federalist era. Having completed recent studies focused on the era of the Vietnam War, Doctor Mrozek plans a book-length essay on US defense policy after World War II.

PREFACE

The Vietnam War stands uneasily on the edge of public memory—slipping into the past and becoming part of our national history, yet still too recent to be forgotten by those who lived through its trials. But history seeks a meaning in its clouded events, a retrospective order and pattern that could instruct, and sometimes even inspire, successive generations. At present, then, Americans face the peculiar dilemma of having to respond to the impact of a war for which there is still no comprehensively shared vision.

One cannot expect broad enthusiasm for a vision of the past whose primary purpose is to justify current policies, acquisitions, deployment, and research. I am reminded here of the adage that, "to be an honest politician, one must first fool oneself before fooling the public." There is much truth in this thought, and it probably applies to many, including historians, defense analysts, and businessmen. The most persuasive visions of the past are the distillations of experience and answers to questions asked in an effort to handle the problems of the present.

The challenge before any society is to maximize the balance between sincerity and accuracy. We need to listen to ourselves—all of us—to our individual thoughts and words, to public statements and pronouncements of policy, and to the less sharply articulated sound of public sentiment. When we hear generalizations about the Vietnam War, we obviously need to ask whether the remarks are valid and ask for the questions behind the questions. In that way, we may isolate the common assumptions which lie behind seemingly conflicting views; and logical analysis may identify the direction in which the myth of Vietnam is moving.

Even though this is only an intermediate step, its effects can be significant. For example, many commentators on the war have described it as heavy on technological ingenuity and weak in human imagination—surely too sweeping a claim, given the remarkable versatility that many men and women showed throughout the war. Yet the common notion that technology received too much emphasis has created a broadly shared interest in reform which is focused on how well we use the weapons we have. What happened to Americans in Vietnam has fostered an inquisitive disposition that was distinctly lacking during the era of "cold war consensus."

Similarly, even though disagreement about who should bear the greatest responsibility for the war's outcome remains keen, it is a widely held understanding that things did not turn out well for the United States, did not show its government in good form, and put inordinate strains on its social fabric. Even without a public admission of failure, military and civilian officials have been able to consider reform for the military and for civil-military interactions to a degree that has been rare in peacetime, reform often focused on human rather than technological questions.

Americans have thought of themselves as individualistic and unruly people—a flattering self-image, though in some ways a false one. Indeed, during the Vietnam War, it was the patience and long-suffering of the American people that most deserved comment. This was not the first war to face great protest and challenge from Americans. Opposition to a massive commitment that was killing young Americans, as well as many Southeast Asians, should hardly have seemed surprising. What should have caused real surprise was how long it took for opposition to coalesce. In the end, the Vietnam experience ought to remind us of how well Americans can rally to a cause, even when it is poorly conceived and executed.

But these are not the lessons of Vietnam. They are only illustrations of how we may come to different understandings of the Vietnam experience. The central lesson is that even when we cannot control the circumstances around us, we can still control ourselves. The use of military and political resources to have our way is not only a practical and technical issue, it is also a philosophical and moral one. It may be worth asking if we have ever won a war by betraying our own traditions and values.

Painful as it was, the Vietnam War was a reminder of the diversity of motivations and interests in the world, as well as the heterogeneity of power. We learned anew that even the very greatest of power centers on earth can never truly monopolize governance of this complex and diverse world. Yet, we need not see the Vietnam experience and its consequences as signs of rot in the framework of national power. They may, in fact, signify only the self-destructiveness and operational inappropriateness of a dualistic cold war mentality whose time has surely passed. What emerges in its place is, as always, entirely up to us.

DONALD J. MROZEK
Senior Research Fellow
Airpower Research Institute

ACKNOWLEDGMENTS

Many of those who were most important in the development of this study will remain unnamed here. Various officers, across the spectrum of rank, contributed to shaping my thoughts on where the Air Force and the military more generally may be heading—or, at least, into what sort of an environment their responsibilities may take them. Yet, because many remain on active service, I am reluctant to enlist either their support or the authority of their experience and expertise on behalf of my arguments. I would be especially loath to do so on matters—including some here—that remain sensitive and occasionally controversial. Nonetheless, my gratitude to them is genuine. And so is my respect. As individuals, the officers who helped me during the course of this study showed a willingness to consider alternative viewpoints, to make real efforts toward interservice cooperation, and to entertain some thoughts that were, by the doctrinal precepts of their own services, "unthinkable." What happens when a diverse body of well-intentioned individuals interoperate in institutions and bureaucracies is, of course, a more complex matter.

The practical preparation of this manuscript was facilitated by the editorial assistance and advice of Preston Bryant and Hugh Richardson of the Air University Press in the Air University Center for Aerospace Doctrine, Research, and Education (AUCADRE) at Maxwell Air Force Base, Alabama. Supervising the physical production of the study was Dorothy McCluskie. The Document Processing Center at AUCADRE, under the direction of Marcia Williams, provided excellent and prompt support; the bulk of the typing and reprocessing was handled by Annie Dinkins, Lula Barnes, and Elaine Dillon. To all who worked so hard and so well to make this work as good as it could be, I owe a real debt; and I appreciate their efforts.

My greatest professional gratitude, however, goes to AUCADRE for providing me the time, support, and encouragement to pursue the concerns which appear in this study. While no question was raised simply for the sake of skepticism, no question was ducked simply for the sake of institutional convenience. No researcher could ask for a more equitable guideline from which to work.

I have chosen to dedicate this study to my nephew, Joseph W. Mrozek III, and to my niece, Dianne Leigh Mrozek. May their world and their future be safer and more humane than ours sometimes seems. May it also be as exciting and as rich with promise.

CHAPTER 1

INTRODUCTION: THE SCOPE OF THE STUDY

> We see things not as they are but as we are.
>
> "Sensation"
> High Museum of Art

This study examines several areas of concern facing the United States Air Force, and the other services in varying degrees, in the years after Vietnam. These concerns are traditional, familiar, and constant when stated abstractly—such matters as doctrine, force structure or "force mix," and professional military education. But this study seeks to find if, how, and to what extent some of these traditional interests may have taken on distinctive features inviting special treatment when considered concretely—in the aftermath of the US involvement in Vietnam. In one sense, the study is not intended as an evaluation of the impact of the US experience in Vietnam in isolation from other influences. In another sense, however, the Vietnam experience affected the US military so deeply and so broadly that it lurks behind most of what has been thought and done in military and security affairs since then, even when civilian or military officials specifically disavow a connection. Vietnam is so much a part of the foundation on which present behavior is premised that it forms part of the context of influence as a matter of fact, even when it is not accepted in this role as a matter of consciousness. To speak, then, of "the Air Force after Vietnam" inevitably entails some assessment of the service's reaction to its experience in the war—good or bad. To speak of the service's "response to its challenges" during the past decade similarly establishes an interplay between the impact of the Vietnam experience and the conscious focus on present difficulties and future contingencies.

To discuss the influence of Vietnam on present behavior requires some stabilization of what the term *Vietnam* encompasses. In the decade since the US withdrawal from South Vietnam and the subsequent collapse of the Saigon regime, the term *Vietnam* has become one of the most fluid, comprehensive, elusive, and enigmatic in US military and political history. Meanings and lessons are hard to tease out of the complexities of the war, largely because lessons and meanings depend on what we seek and how we choose to evaluate rather than on anything intrinsic to events in Southeast

Asia. Moreover, to the extent that Americans retain the illusion of their own pragmatism in world affairs, as if they escaped having an ideology simply because they dislike using the word, it remains difficult even to identify pertinent goals toward which operations in Vietnam could have been devoted and against which they could have been credibly evaluated. To the extent that goals and means thus become reciprocal and equal, action loses its sense of direction—and later analysis of that action becomes incurably ambiguous. The ambiguity of Vietnam is, indeed, its primary and dominant feature. It is a war that was not quite a war by customary US standards. It showed Americans at their best and at their worst, although which Americans fall into which category is itself a matter of opinion. It divided Americans as few wars before it, yet it united and recombined various clusters and groups of Americans who had previously held apart from each other. It was made up of a string of US victories, but the victories lacked tangible rewards. Moral victories could produce more tangible results, but those accrued more typically to the other side. Given the contingency of the values with which we might evaluate the war, and given the complexity of the war on its own terms, it is doubtful that any "true and comprehensive picture" of Vietnam will ever develop—at least none with clear lines, sharp contrasts, and all the nuances of hue and shading. If it remains complex and ambiguous, Vietnam may influence Americans in much the way the American Civil War continues to affect them. That something may be learned and gained from it is possible, even though there will never be any perfect resolution of the conflict in values that inspired the war in the first place. Although it is a war of which one cannot expect to say, "When all is said and done," we reach a point where enough is said so that we look for the residue beyond the continuing flow of words. In the end, perhaps the phrase most pertinent will not be "the horror of Vietnam" but "the horror of uncertainty."

The foregoing remarks do not outline the meaning of the word *Vietnam* in a precise way. But they may underscore, at least, that Vietnam is more than a place, more than a war, more than a lesson. Rather, it is a vortex of numerous competing concerns, a double-edged memory that prunes our ambitions yet feeds them with our emotions. And it was the instrument of destruction with which Americans savaged their own vision of a bipolar world conflict. The "challenge of Vietnam," by extension, has become the task of meeting usual, though serious, obligations while still being affected by assumptions rooted in a quite different vision of the world situation.

On the other hand, there are significant issues that originate in conditions not primarily driven by the Vietnam experience. Matters of doctrine and force structure, for example, are rooted in the historical development of the military services themselves and in the evolution of a mechanism aimed at coordinating their efforts. Notwithstanding their deep grounding in historical experience, which far exceeds American contact with South Vietnam, the more recent developments in doctrine, force structure, and other such matters have been at least obliquely affected by Vietnam.

Any experience fraught with difficulty can make people wish simply to forget about it, but ignoring an experience without resolving its implications and extended impact is dangerous. If the issues raised by the manner and outcome of US involvement in Vietnam were to remain unsettled, the memory of Vietnam would be like a nasty neighborhood dog repeatedly nipping at one's heels. Lasting peace and common sense argue in favor of noticing that the dog is there because, even though what some would see as an unsettling "dog" of a war has only limited force of its own, it could make one do foolish things. The unpopularity not only of Vietnam itself but of giving it serious postmortem attention may stem largely from its obvious beginning; and all participants seek to escape allegations of parentage while seeing visible signs that their own roles in that nasty war became perverse parodies of the truth.

In some measure, the avoidance of Vietnam and its dismissal as having no valid implications and lessons for the military and the nation after the mid-1970s may owe much to the war's nastiness, complexity, and its outcome. Casual conversation among military professionals in the years after the fall of Saigon included such comments as this of Saigon included such comments as this synthesis drawn from numerous specific cases: "That war was such a screwed-up mess that I'm not even going to talk about it—or think about it—anymore." Such "forgetting" may also have its utilitarian aspects; "remembering," for example, might lead to a fundamental reexamination of missions and tactics or to strengthening a case for large adjustments in force structure. For the Air Force, however, the more relevant source of disinterest in Vietnam may have to do with its own rather distinctive relationship to history. Some observers of Air Force officers, comparing them with those in the other services, have pointed to their particularly strong technological bent. Edward Marks, for example, a foreign service officer who had met members of all the services while he was a student at the National War College, said that "the Air Force types were quick and clever but tended to be narrow and obsessed with gadgetry. . . ."[1] From a slightly different vantage, an observer could see this same characteristic as a diminished sense of history. Although all armed forces necessarily care about technology in the contemporary world, the Air Force owes its very origin to a special combination of technological developments at a time when the future was deemed unusually more relevant than the past. Of course, the airmen did not even have a past to draw on. To be sure, long cultural development does not explain behavior decades later, especially not in some mechanistic way, but nuances of disposition still help to set one's agenda except when external pressure of a commanding sort dictates it.

We have long been inclined, as a people, to be fascinated by images of the future, and this tendency has shown itself in our military consciousness where we are understandably interested in future possibilities that may affect security. But perhaps we have cultivated a greater sense of fundamental novelty than is justifiable; a measure of skepticism might be useful. Perhaps we should think that the future will be just like the past—only more so. After all, revolutionary transformations have been very few. Incremental change is more common and more likely; and major changes, when they do come, are usually associated with a transformation in our disposition to accept change. Even Vietnam, despite its enormous impact on the United States, stands as an incremental extension of America's thinking about war.

But there is another side to the coin, and it is related to the avoidance of Vietnam that some sought to maintain. Vietnam has at times been used as a whipping boy to explain difficulties whose causes may have been much more varied. In turn, some specific parties, such as Congress, have become special targets. The very ambiguity and complexity of Vietnam have permitted a considerable measure of "finger pointing"—attributing failure in our broadest objectives to the manifest shortcomings of others. This study, given its relative brevity and its attempt to touch on a wide range of interconnected issues, cannot provide an exhaustive treatment of the "Vietnam syndrome." It seeks only to give a rough map of varied assessments, perhaps enabling us to appreciate how an apparently disciplined forward movement can turn into a dangerous and even fatal false step.

The point here is not to assert that a particular interpretation of Vietnam and the Vietnam syndrome ought to become the basis on which policies are enunciated. Instead, the point is that Vietnam is an "open metaphor"—available to virtually any user in almost any context. Vietnam proves nothing in particular and can be used for virtually everything. Vietnam is a piano; the sound that it produces is up to the composer and the player. Whether celebration or dirge, triumph or tragedy—it is all up to the user.

Notes

1. Edward Marks, "Letter from Fort McNair," *Foreign Service Journal* 60, no. 2 (February 1983): 30.

CHAPTER 2

VIETNAM IN HISTORY

Every war—and every peace—soon becomes a part of written, spoken, changing history. Vietnam is no exception. Any single work about a major undertaking is, of course, a fixed object; yet the ideas contained within it may be flexible and pliable, triggering new thoughts and inviting reinterpretation of the original event. Even more complex and rich with potential meanings is the event itself; despite its having been a discrete "something" at its occurrence, it takes on extraordinary versatility when subjected to imaginative human reexamination. Nor is this play of the original event against the interests of later investigators an impeachment of the latters' motives or methods, for there is an abiding truth to Carl Becker's suggestion several decades ago that "every man is his own historian."[1] Each brings special concerns and questions; and the richness of the actual event itself unfolds only in pieces or parts, teased out in response to what has been asked.

This flexibility of events and their interpretation is not a result of insufficient information, premature appraisal, or other shortcomings. It lies in the inherent diversity of events and of the people who make them happen. Similarly, these characteristics do not necessarily apply more heavily to the recent past than to much earlier experience. For example, it is hardly scarcity of attention or weakness of scholarship that accounts for continuing discussion of the meaning and impact of the American Civil War. Instead, periodic shifts of concern within contemporary society open new angles of vision toward battles long past and toward their consequences.[2] Often heroic in tone, the writing devoted to the Civil War soon after its conclusion served something much greater than a romantic appetite; it marked a struggle between proponents of a highly professional and well-trained armed force relatively larger than had been traditional in the United States on the one hand and advocates of the militia spirit on the other. Who had performed more valiantly in the late war—regulars or volunteers drawn from the state manpower pools? The issue had unmistakable political connotations.[3] In matters of social policy as well as military theory and organization, the evolving literature on the Civil War was substantially conditioned by interests contemporary with the writers, even though they dealt with events of a steadily receding past. The questioning of the constitutional legitimacy of the war itself suggested a perceptible shift of responsibility—or, to anticipate a more extreme term, *war guilt*—away from the confederacy and its "peculiar institution" of slavery. Coming at a time when the South was beginning its reassertion of political power on the national as well as regional scene (which was soon exemplified by the election of Virginia-born Woodrow Wilson to the presidency), the romantic reexamination of the Civil War past was not without its contributions to the turn-of-the-century present.[4]

Nor does the United States hold a monopoly on the sort of flexible examination of past wars that assuages curiosities born of contemporary interests. The special interpretation the French gave of their disastrous defeat in the Franco-Prussian War serves as one illustration. Placing tremendous emphasis on a failure of nerve, and convinced of the crucial importance of what philosopher Henri Bergson called élan vital, or vital spirit, the French emphasized motivation and enthusiasm at the expense of more mundane method and detail. The final cost was calculated in French dead and in near defeat in World War I.[5] Similarly, the assessment of the origins and conduct of World War I had tremendous impact on military affairs between the two world wars; and it is generally conceded that the revisionist historical interpretation, driven partly by sympathy for the German public struggling with inflation and war reparation payments, finally contributed to the remilitarization of Germany and the prospects of war.[6]

History, then, is a tool for understanding and a weapon for advancing policy. This is no novelty and should occasion no surprise, but it may be difficult to hold the line between history and advocacy when dealing with sensitive events relatively close to the present. Nonetheless, distinguishing between the two—in one's own conscience as well as in one's assessment of the efforts of others—means the difference between benefiting from error and setting the stage for committing new ones.

Unfortunately, claiming that one has learned something does not mean that it has actually happened. Again, the case of Vietnam is not exceptional. Even those who have thought hard about a war do not necessarily gain a new appreciation of it—too much depends on what assumptions they carried into their retrospect, what outcomes were consciously or unconsciously sought, and many other considerations that distort the process and prejudice its results. Nor do personal experience and authority drawn from high rank ensure insight into events in which one was a participant. Some hint of the limits of the learning process may be gained from remarks offered by former Secretary of Defense Robert S. McNamara. In an interview with *Washington Post* writer Paul Hendrickson, McNamara said he knew even in the 1960s that Vietnam had lessons to offer. "I knew as early as 1966 there were lessons to be learned," McNamara said in 1984. "Of course I did. I started the Pentagon Papers and goddammit, that's why I did it," he added. But the limits of McNamara's learning were revealed in his next remark, offered parenthetically: "I never read the Pentagon Papers, by the way."[7] Merely initiating a bureaucratic process of assembling the data and bringing them into some preliminary historical order did not automatically constitute learning. Since what one can learn is delimited in some measure by what one already thinks, the Pentagon Papers were in themselves merely a data base; and the judgments and lessons contained in them represented little more than indexing systems. Precisely what should have been done could not be determined from the Pentagon Papers alone—the value system of each reader was required. Thus, McNamara's sense of satisfaction at initiating the process that produced the Pentagon Papers had a rather hollow ring.

Others, including Hendrickson, proved less sanguine about the ease and decisiveness with which one might learn from the experience of Vietnam. "Vietnam is our great myth now," Hendrickson wrote in May 1984. "It has superseded every other twentieth century American fable. What makes it so terrible a tragedy and fine a myth is its impenetrability." Showing little of the clipped assurance of McNamara, Hendrickson continued: "It is a puzzle without pieces, a riddle without rhyme. How could it have gone so wrong, all those lost American lives, nearly 60,000? And who was the enemy, exactly?"[8] Sooner or later, those dealing with the nation's affairs had to deal with the concerns and problems addressed by those questions. How they did so—with what kind of consciousness, with what sort of intent, and with what type of methodology—set out the parameters within which Vietnam could take on enduring public meaning.

The Continuing Relevance of the Vietnam Era

The relevance of the Vietnam experience depends, in part, on the agenda of those studying it. The special risk for the military is tied to the importance of doctrine, a consciously advanced and sharply articulated ideology of military affairs. In such a context, learning teeters at the brink of submission to doctrine; unbiased learning is badly jeopardized. Historical events are mustered to validate doctrinal propositions. The emphasis on vocabulary, such as the word *validate*, is far more than an academic exercise in semantics—it underscores a particular way of using the past that contradicts the essential complexity of history. The mere construction of a process whereby historical experience is employed to validate a doctrine implicitly asserts that doctrine is the constant and that events are subordinate. In such a circumstance, experience risks becoming a footnote on theory and concrete events risk being turned into servants of abstract formulations.[9]

Although this knotty relationship between history and theory extends to all forms of discourse, the conscious attention to military doctrine makes the tension especially clear within the armed services. In the emergence of studies on the Vietnam era by serving or retired officers, an inevitable interplay developed between doctrinal heritage (itself understood largely as the synthesis of historical experience) and the seeming challenges posed by events of the recent past. A primary test of military relevance for the Vietnam era, then, seemed to reside in the reciprocity of recent events with doctrine. If the events could be so understood as to support existing doctrine, then there might be little about them especially worth remembering. On the other hand, if the events violated the predicted results of prevailing doctrine, it might be necessary to attribute failures to improper conduct, of both operations and the war as a whole, thus validating doctrine by invalidating experience. Perhaps most subtly, it was possible to embrace the past within the framework of one's own deep-seated beliefs and inclinations. Without dishonesty, one might still see falsely; and the product of one's peculiar vision of experience would enjoy internal consistency yet stand as something of an "intellectual Black Mass."[10]

Notwithstanding such risks, however, analysis of past events, including recent and unpleasant ones, is imperative. Sooner or later, they have consequences whether examined or not. Thus, whether directly or through its effects, the armed services would inevitably deal with Vietnam. Given the immense impact on US military personnel and resources, on public tolerance and the politico-military system, and on a wide range of other things, logic militated in favor of dealing with it frontally. Arguably the most badly savaged service arm, the Army was the first to take the war into its corporate memory; and it produced what were, in many ways, the most ingratiating early works on the military aspects of the Vietnam experience. The Department of the Army produced the Vietnam Studies, topically organized volumes on such matters as logistics or intelligence and issued under the name of two- and three-star US generals. Indochina Monographs, providing firsthand accounts by high-ranking Vietnamese and Laotian officers, were issued by the Army's Center of Military History, which also produced the Army's official history. One of the most appealing qualities of both series was their businesslike, essentially noncontroversial, reserved, and professional tone. They seemed to come closer than other public efforts at the time to beginning a sound descriptive assessment of the war on the firm basis of military science. In time, the Army's histories could be turned into a comprehensive vision of the Vietnam experience—one distinguished by its grasp toward the principles of war rather than the principles of sea power, air power, or land power. The reasonableness in tone of these writings, and the breadth of their integration, put the Army in a favorable position for influencing the emerging understanding of what had happened in Southeast Asia.[11]

The actual content of these studies, however, could not have been completely neutral or value-free. Would it have been realistic to imagine that the pre-Vietnam experience and the doctrinal, strategic, and policy interests of the authors could have been bred out of these works? And had it been possible, would it even have been a virtue? Whatever the answer to the most speculative of these notions, the books themselves had interpretative implications well beyond the seeming confines of operational history. The works provided substantial support for the view that the details of US operations in Vietnam had been handled with substantial—sometimes consummate—skill. In studies of logistic support and of riverine operations, for example, the keynote was the record of achievement of well-trained forces in extremely difficult circumstances. Similarly, the extraordinary performance of medical support teams, coupled with improvements in medical treatment, was shown to have reduced the likelihood of battlefield death.[12] One might well have wondered why, if all these many particulars were handled so well, the final result was poor.

Nor was this general line of approach restricted to support services or to special action units. Retired Army Gen Donn A. Starry, for example, spoke with enthusiasm on the use of armor in Vietnam by the United States, showing genuine pride that armor operations proved possible over a far greater percentage of the country than had first been expected.[13] Calculating the actual worth of such armor operations surely remained one of the most ambiguous of undertakings; but Starry did not share the sense of doubt. A representative curiosity in Starry's approach was the praise given to Rome plows fixed to tractors and bulldozers pressing through jungles and clearing access routes and landing zones. Lauding the swiftness of movement through the vegetation took on a particularly odd note when compared with the standard of swiftness associated with airmobility. Similarly intriguing assessments can be found in Gen Bernard Rogers's study on Operations Cedar Falls and Junction City, which he pronounced a clear success. In both cases, however, even though the authors claimed real tactical and possible strategic gains, the rock-bottom source of pride was in professional accomplishment—in the efficacy of the forces, in the soundness of both men and machines, in the basic strength of leadership throughout the combat units.[14]

The cumulative lesson of all such works hinted at particular directions where things might have gone wrong. Most of the traces seemed to lead toward questions of policy and strategy, and the premises on which both were made at the highest level. At the highest policy levels, there was a hint of uncertainty—of insufficient clarity in goals to pursue and means of pursuing them. And at the highest level of military leadership, there may have been too great a sense of novelty and too little an insistence on professional judgment and experience. Anticipating views soon to be expounded by serving officers, Dave Richard Palmer pressed these implications in *Summons of the Trumpet*.[15] In the aftermath of the Korean War, the Army had concluded in its 1954 field service regulations that since "wars of limited objective" were now possible, "victory" was no longer the categorical objective of combat. Thus, using an absolute and extreme definition of victory, the outcome of Korea constituted no victory even if it had met the basic requirements of the United States and the United Nations. This in turn fostered the false impression that so-called limited war was abnormal and that "total war," actually quite unusual, was normative. This misapprehension, along with the impeachment of professional military judgment and past military history itself, contributed to the prospects for disaster. Gradually, the accumulation of testimonies to the efficiency of various units in Vietnam defied the outcome of the war as a whole and laid claim once again to the authoritativeness of military judgment. It was not without ultimate significance and effect on the US military that this case for military judgment was spearheaded from the perspective of one service with seemingly greater force than from the others. In some uncertain measure, it was a question of coming to grips with the war, but it was also a question of coming to a vision of the character of warfare in general and of representing that particular vision as the basis for common interservice preparations for future defense. Intended or not, the final stakes comprised capturing the myth of Vietnam and, with it, the future of defense. Whose predispositions and doctrinal heritage would most powerfully mold the meaning into which Vietnam would be fitted?

The Emergence of History and Advocacy

The installation of views that had grown gradually within the Army as a credible basis for national defense and general strategic planning was suggested by the considerable public interest won by Harry Summers's *On Strategy: The Vietnam War in Context*.[16] For popular audiences, Summers offered the same concise judgment on Vietnam. "What I point out in the book," he told an interviewer for *Parade* magazine in 1983, "is what James Madison, Alexander Hamilton, and Carl von Clausewitz pointed out long ago. No government should commit troops to battle without first obtaining solid public support and carefully delineating its war objectives. We failed to do that in Vietnam." Summers also gave popular and professional readers the same message concerning possible future undertakings, and there were unmistakable implications for current and future policy. In fact, the limits imposed on the effectiveness of military operations by the characteristics of the American political-military system seemed to suggest that the anticipated constraints on performance should force reexamination of objectives. Suggesting the need for caution in accepting new obligations, he added: "If the majority of the American people don't want their armed forces to fight in Nicaragua, El Salvador or Lebanon, then we shouldn't fight there." Citing "fundamental limitations" on the use of US military power, especially against an insurrection in a foreign state, he warned that "once we send our troops to fight on foreign soil, we frequently aggravate the problem instead of solving it. Our intervention becomes counterproductive."[17]

On first glance, Summers appeared to join the chorus of voices seeing the US effort in Vietnam as inherently wrongheaded and doomed to failure on grounds that it violated the popular spirit of the Vietnamese and, eventually, of the Americans as well. But after further reflection, and especially after a closer look at the elaboration of argument behind the generalizations, a far less critical or questioning line of thought emerged. Summers not only indicted high-level policymakers and executors for lack of clarity during the Vietnam War but also suggested that the basis for a clear—and effective—policy actually existed. He asserted boldly that the government in Hanoi managed the "other side" during the war, reducing to nearly marginal significance any autonomy that might have existed among dissident South Vietnamese. This matter requires much consideration in its own right; but as a preliminary assessment, one may take note of the ultimately comforting and reassuring quality of a critique that tends to provide a unitary explanation for the behavior of one's opponents. At first blush, it must seem difficult to write a book that will please many about a war that pleased few; and so the considerable currency of Summers's book occasions notice.[18] But the greater truth may be that dissatisfaction with the war preconditioned a large audience to accept critical remarks. Criticism of operational techniques or of their relationship to some larger strategic scheme could be swallowed if traditional doctrinal directions were not recharted. And it would surely prove relatively easy to accept such criticism within the Army if the doctrine that won implicit reaffirmation was its own. In the end, such implications did flow from Summers's work, which was an uncompromising call for a return to traditional principles of war, for a rejection of novelties as if they were for their own sake, for a renewed use of professional military judgment, and for a wide range of other propositions. But the implications of such views might become knottier: What if it turned out to be a theoretically attractive and emotionally appealing interpretation, but one that reflected only a few selected aspects of the war and met only selected features of the contemporary world it sought to serve?

The suitable point of departure must lie within Summers's argument itself. He notes that various US officials asserted that there was a serious indigenous insurgency in South Vietnam and suggests that they deceived themselves by thinking of the war as a fundamentally or even exclusively local problem. But such a view—and even a much less extreme version of it—is not borne out in the abundant records available from National Security Council meetings, cabinet meetings, presidential advisers of both the Kennedy and Johnson administrations, and other sources. Whatever errors were committed by both civilian and military advisers to the president, assuming that the insurgents in the South were either independent or substantially free of the North Vietnamese was not among them.[19]

Walt Rostow's judgment that the North was deeply at fault—and that its involvement was essential to continuing disorder in the South—raised the prospect of having to deploy forces across the Ho Chi Minh trail system, from northwestern South Vietnam below the DMZ out into Laos. Early on, limited aircraft deployment and limited use of aerial firepower were explicitly intended as symbolic statements to Hanoi and not as measures through which specific and direct military gains would be made against the insurgents in the South. When "graduated response" did in fact graduate, when escalation and geographical redirection of bombing took place, it was not because of a sudden epiphany that Hanoi was somewhat involved but as a somewhat despairing measure justified by the evident insufficiency of earlier US "symbolic communication" with North Vietnam. If speaking through air power in Laos proved insufficient or if positioning US naval forces in close proximity to North Vietnam proved inaudible, then perhaps it was necessary to use harsher words and to shout. So, ultimately, did a logic aimed at persuasion of the leadership in Hanoi emerge; but it was focused, even from its earliest and quite modest origins, on North Vietnam. Indeed, one could page without end through the documents piled up from White House and executive office building personnel and find precious little about specifically southern insurgents.[20]

Far more knotty for US officials was the weaving of a path between constraints imposed by domestic interests and those imposed by external forces. Real limits still existed as to what the United States could do without incurring unacceptable political damage overseas during a passionately anticolonialist period and without generating unreasonable pressures within the United States. It became fashionable to say that Johnson restrained and hampered the US commitment in Vietnam out of fear that he would damage his Great Society program. But the "revolution of rising expectations" that was cited as an explanation for unrest overseas applied to the United States as well. The constraints were considerable and genuine.[21]

Particularly at a time when limited war theories were in season, limited methods had an aura of legitimacy. This, too, has been portrayed as something of a defect; but what was the practical alternative? The catchphrase was that Johnson and his advisers confused limited war with limited commitment. Yet, presuming that even identifiable and clear goals are not always worth risking all of one's resources, how does one draw the line? Realistically and practically, what would unlimited commitment have meant in a limited war for less than live-or-die stakes?[22]

Although US leaders were aware that Hanoi was deeply involved, the issue was how to do something about it without damaging other US interests. To say that the United States must have blinded itself to Hanoi's role in the South and to imply justification for the argument on grounds that US military means were constrained would be somewhat like trying to prove that, in the 1980s, the United States saw no links between terrorist acts and certain national governmental authorities. The imagined "proof" that would be required would be, for example, that the United States had failed to bomb Tehran. It would be like suggesting that the United States saw no ties between regional and local problems on the one hand and the Soviet Union and Cuba on the other. The issue lies in determining the costs of doing something about it as well as the chances of doing it successfully. The neat perception of Vietnam as a simple binary conflict took the war after the Tet offensive of 1968 as the true version, impeaching the importance of the war's multitrack, multilevel structure in earlier years. It was part of an interpretative turn away from counterinsurgency, as if counterinsurgency were merely theory rather than a centuries-old recurrent phenomenon; and it was an embrace of the conventional armed force wisdom of the pre-Vietnam days. This specialized version of the war held great potential for influencing strategic thinking, forecasting possible and probable forms of conflict, and developing preferences in force structure. The honor and wisdom of past events were the immediate subjects at issue, but the prize was the future.[23]

Still, the basic argument suffers not only from a certain measure of inaccuracy but also from a measure of inconsistency. Summers simultaneously dismisses the notion of independent insurgents in South Vietnam while proposing that insurgent groups operate with substantial independence and seek to avoid overdependence on supplies and guidance from outside the zone of conflict. One is forced to wonder why it should be necessary to protect South Vietnam from external intrusion so as to let the local government's forces suppress the local insurgents if there were no local insurgents. Nor can it be that the problems are all imported from outside, as Summers himself clearly knows. His own critique of the US military role in nation-building and civic action clearly exposes the fact that the government in Saigon was not undertaking that critical task effectively and, by necessary implication, was as much of a problem as Hanoi—whether in prosecuting a war against the insurgents or in managing war at other levels. Here, in the end, was a government incapable of reforming itself even when the cost was a lethal threat to the survival of South Vietnam's "national" identity. Even at a distance of several years, it is difficult to determine precisely what strategy would have transformed Saigon's government sufficiently for it to gain genuine control and authority over South Vietnam.[24]

Specific treatment of the Tet offensive of 1968 also raises logical questions.[25] How is it that the conflict in the South was without its indigenous element if one of Hanoi's alleged interests in staging the Tet offensive was to wipe out local leaders in the South? If the latter was part of the plan, then Hanoi must have assumed that there indeed were indigenous insurgents in the South. And even if Hanoi did not believe it, the allegation itself remains logically incompatible with simultaneous assertions that the problems in the South were predominantly imported from the North.

A further problem resident in the methodology is a willingness to accept the post-1975 statements of North Vietnamese about their conduct of the war and their intentions while discounting so many of their statements made during the war itself. It is as if the leadership in Hanoi ceased having any political reasons to constrain candor simply because they had won. Logically, there is no reason to assume that a regime which had practical interests in describing events in ways ranging from eccentric to completely false during the war would instantly be deprived of those interests and motivations on the collapse of an adversary. For some US writers, after all, the Vietnam War was over. Indeed, some regarded it as "over" in 1973, let alone 1975. For the Vietnamese, however, despite the collapse of the Saigon regime and the removal of the Americans, other pieces in the larger Indochina conflict continued—and still continue. Thus, what was becoming a matter of historical retrospect in Washington was still largely a matter of current events in Hanoi.

The view of the Vietnam War emerging in some quarters seemed driven less by events in Indochina than by current visions of the character of warfare. In one sense and in one set of categories, this could be useful and even laudable. A particular case that did not lend itself to general principles would surely be anomalous—and unlikely. Yet the danger lay in reading into the past a currently preferable way of warfighting. In the case of Summers, for example, as with some of the highest Army leaders of the last decade, there developed a surprisingly strong cautionary attitude that there were, indeed, some wars that the United States should sit out.[26] Carried into the past, however, this seemed to warp Vietnam. An imaginary version of how the war might conceivably have been won emerged while the tactics and doctrine actually used in Vietnam were criticized as having been ill-suited to some largely imaginary conditions.

An additional intriguing aspect of this emerging quasi-official military version of the Vietnam War is the degree to which it departs from previous testimonies as to the war's character, even by a good many military officers including some of high rank.[27] The discrepancies between Summers's view and that of General Starry, for example, are instructive. In *Mounted Combat in Vietnam*, General Starry accepted that there had been a genuinely local side to the war in which dissident groups constituted an important resource for an insurgency.[28] In this way, General Starry avoided the problem of confusing *whether* there would have been conflict without aid and coordination from Hanoi with *what kind* of conflict might have been sustained without them.

The contemporary utility of such an interpretation of Vietnam was that it discouraged attention to a host of unhappy aspects of current problems. It invited viewing each conflict in a larger sense, which was much more comfortable for traditionalists in the military services to deal with. It encouraged attending to wars of higher intensity, which also had the luxury of being the wars least likely to be fought (such as a conflict in Europe or a nuclear war). Thus, interpreting Vietnam in falsely neat terms supported the focusing of maximum attention on wars of least likelihood while suggesting minimum accommodation for wars of greatest probability. This, surely, is eccentric respect for Clausewitz. For although the Prussian theorist was right in proclaiming the need to avoid being swamped by the sheer dynamics of war, he was especially right in seeing that the objective had to be the *proper* one.

Even as assessments of war in progress govern the strategy to be pursued, retrospective analyses of a war determine current and future policy. Achieving a *proper* vision—accurate and relevant—is the object of the whole exercise. In a lighter vein than he would likely have sustained in a different forum, Summers commented on a review of his book *On Strategy* in a way that occasioned question as to the accuracy of his approach. He sought to compare the South Vietnamese posture after 1954–56 with the southerners' stereotypical vision of the American Civil War as a "War for Southern Independence." This perhaps playful but certainly peculiar comparison exemplified the tendency to portray the Vietnam War largely as a conventional war between two opposing nation-states aided by their respective allies and, at least in one case, bolstered by a substantial "fifth column" within the aggrieved state. Seeking to pass off the criticisms lodged against his arguments by Professor Gerald Berkeley of Auburn University at Montgomery, Alabama, Summers misread Berkeley's conclusion that "we need to be more accurate in our assessment of the type of situation we are facing." Summers interpreted that to mean the process of assessment is more important than the accuracy of its results. The issue is not whether strategic vision must be kept sharp and clear, but whether Summers's reading of Vietnam encourages false policy by offering false lessons.[29]

Vantage Points and Visions

While an interpretation of Vietnam premised on the traditional principles of war was gradually taking shape among various Army officers and historians, certain Air Force publications tended to place a greater emphasis on the principles of air power and on the proper role of air power in contemporary wars. The other services were less prompt than the Army in beginning to frame observations about the war on the bedrock of military thought and practice. Different vantage points afforded different visions. Some works that appeared early—in some cases, even while the war was still under way—seemed more likely to motivate heroic performance than to serve as the foundation for a comprehensive understanding of the war. Two examples are *Aces & Aerial Victories: The United States Air Force in Southeast Asia, 1965-1973* issued in 1976 by the Air Force's Albert F. Simpson Historical Research Center and the Office of Air Force History, and *Seven Firefights in Vietnam*, released in 1970 by the Army's Office of the Chief of Military History.[30] Others touched on high-visibility events, such as the fight at Khe Sanh, providing a measure of praise for the professionalism of the combat forces involved and staking some implied claim to responsibility for the successful outcome.[31] Such works were never intended as enduring and all-encompassing official histories; they were preliminary essays into what promised to be a vast undertaking.

Even then, the services were engaged in efforts to save and assemble material to document the war, including interviews with senior officers, after action and end of tour reports, and a variety of other items. Eventually, the first works in the official history of the war written by the respective services began to appear. From the Navy's historical branch came Edwin Brickford Hooper, Dean C. Allard, and Oscar P. Fitzgerald's *The United States Navy in the Vietnam Conflict*, volume 1, *The Setting of the Stage to 1959*; from the Marine Corps, the first volumes in their operational history such as Jack Shulimson's *U.S. Marines in Vietnam, 1966: An Expanding War*; and the first volume of the Air Force official history, *The Advisory Years to 1965*, drafted by Robert Frank Futrell and revised by Martin Blumenson.[32] In addition, specialized studies appeared under the aegis of the Office of Air Force History on topics such as the development on fixed-wing gunships and defoliation.[33]

The most significant of the works appearing in the 1970s, however, may have been some that skirted the edge of official history—essentially memoirs. Standing out for attention among these are William W. Momyer's *Air Power in Three Wars* and U. S. Grant Sharp's *Strategy for Defeat, Vietnam in Retrospect*.[34] Momyer's work affirmed the postulates of air power as developed in the 1920s and 1930s with relatively brief comments on World War II, asserted the enduring validity of these precepts by reference to the Korean War, and associated the shortcomings of the Vietnam conflict with failure to follow the principles of air power. Largely a memoir of his service in Vietnam as commander of the Seventh Air Force and as Gen William C. Westmoreland's air deputy, the work created an aura which was at once defensive and challenging—defensive in the sense that it implicitly argued against charges that air power, and especially the Air Force, had failed in Vietnam, and challenging in that it sought to rally readers in support of a more traditional view that had been put in limbo by counterinsurgency and theories about limited war.³⁵

But there was a message running between the lines that kept saying, "I told you so." The restatement of air power postulates, which had already had effective doctrinal force for half a century, limited the range of alternative creative thinking and made the importance of air power and of the Air Force, more than the relationship of air power to the basic principles of war, the focus. Whatever the intention, much of the effect was to extend the justifying argument for a separate Air Force and to continue the traditional Air Force quest for the "unity of air power." Even if true, such postulates lacked sufficient extensiveness to touch the concerns of all the major "warrior constituencies." Thus, irrespective of accuracy, they courted irrelevance in some important quarters.

Part of the problem was in the implicit logic that, since what was done in Vietnam did not promptly conform to the precepts of air power and since it failed to achieve the final US objectives, then adoption of those precepts would have worked. For those who already believed in the doctrinal postulates of air power, an argument running on the edge of such assumptions was not only acceptable but reassuring; and there was something to be said for rallying to the task at hand with a minimum of self-criticism lest it become self-doubt. But since the possible military obligations of the United States ranged widely over the spectrum of intensity and since the gradual historical appraisal of Vietnam took substantial notice of the war's complexity, a monolithic interpretation of the war and a doctrinally neat specification of how it could have been remedied resembled simplism and special pleading.³⁶ Whether right or wrong, such an approach may have been a bit impolitic. If one already believed such an argument, this was a strong statement of it; but if one was not already persuaded, it risked seeming tendentious.

Like General Momyer, Admiral Sharp attended keenly to the shortcomings of the war's conduct and drew heavily on his own professional experience to support what he believed would have been a strategy for victory. But such a hypothesis was ultimately beyond testing; and his categorical claim for the validity of his view stripped it of an objective appearance. Transparent contempt for certain figures, such as Robert McNamara, had a disabling effect. It seemed nearly to reduce the war to a duel between different kinds of expertise—a flirtation with the logical fallacy of argument from authority.³⁷

The actual merits of Momyer's and Sharp's views are not the pertinent matter here. Rather, it is the question of how those views were presented and how the manner of presentation may have restricted the acceptability of their messages. The style may have become the substance of the message projected, alienating some from Momyer and Sharp and their doctrinal inclinations. It is not enough to be right if one is also distant.

Principles or Preferences

The principles of war are basically only special expressions of the principles of human behavior. Emphasis on a particular principle and the concrete meaning attached to the generally stated form of a principle are likely to suggest some measure of preference—some underlying agenda. A simplified history—that is, the making of references to the past—has always obtained in modern societies. But the balance between principle, preference, and historical precedent is elusive; and traditions, biases, and doctrinal predispositions are difficult to breed out of one's application of a generally accepted principle. The common talk about possible war and provisions for defense after the mid-1970s played into a shadowland where all truth wore a cloak of gray.

Among the shades were some that held many in their sway. Some ideas that fell out during postwar reaction and reflection harmonized with traditional professional norms and expectations. They were easily acceptable to the officer corps; yet they sounded uncommon enough to seem, falsely, that they had been driven especially by Vietnam. But the manner of response, in the end, was a skip back into the cadence of perspectives that were anchored solidly in tradition. *New York Times Magazine* military writer Drew Middleton, for example, thought that the memories of Vietnam were still eating away at many who had served in Southeast Asia. In "Vietnam and the Military Mind," published in the *Times Magazine* on 10 January 1982, Middleton said that memories of Vietnam were "still painfully fresh," feeding the "bitter conviction that, had things been run differently, the war could have been won."[38] Although Army officers, for example, did seek to gain some lessons from their Southeast Asian experience, Middleton pointed to the military's "deep, abiding resentment" at how the war was reported.[39] The military's assessment of its own professional performance tended to focus on practical matters such as the need for clear policy, personnel procedures, and logistical support; its assessment of outside parties, including the electronic media, remained broad and inclusive, ultimately contributing to the view that the media were more responsible for the failure in Vietnam than the military were. Developing a composite from his discussions with officers from the several services, Middleton described the judgment the military had on Vietnam: "Too much effort, he was sure, was being expended on sideshows, such as programs designed to 'win more hearts and minds' of the South Vietnamese. Give the Army and Air Force their head, he would say, and victory would win more hearts and minds than any land reform or village-resettlement program."[40] The media, the political leadership, and antiwar activists were among those considered suspect—as having discouraged relying on the professional military in establishing the ground rules of the war. In this way, the military might determine that the Vietnam experience was not really their own defeat after all, laying it instead at several civilian doorsteps. As to broader lessons, the evaluation might proceed with less vigor, overcome by visions inspired by deep-seated presuppositions about the nature of war and American preferences for its conduct.

The larger point, however, was to establish a suitable basis for future performance. In this regard, Army officers made no secret of their diffidence as to US military involvement overseas in the 1980s, evidently seeking to clarify terms and encourage both broader awareness and some consensus on what might likely be done. Reporting in the *New York Times Magazine* on 21 June 1983, Drew Middleton wrote of the "unusual unanimity" with which senior Army generals opposed US military intervention in Central America "without the clear, unequivocal support of Congress and the people."[41] Among those specifically mentioned were Gen John W. Vessey, Jr., chairman of the Joint Chiefs of Staff; Gen Edward C. Meyer, then Army chief of staff; Gen Wallace Nutting, former Southern Command head, then with Readiness Command; Gen Bernard W. Rogers, supreme commander of NATO; and Gen William C. Westmoreland, US commander in Vietnam during the war. Middleton emphasized that military officers saw Central American problems as complex and integrated—economic, political, social, and military—problems that cannot be solved by a restrictively or even predominantly military effort. Some officers, whose names Middleton did not provide, warned that sending even one American brigade to El Salvador would "push the peasants toward the leftist insurgents." They insisted that the goal of policy be clear and that the American public be given a clear picture on risks and costs in money and manpower. In an intriguing variant on the principles underlying the War Powers Act of 1973, General Westmoreland suggested that any congressional authorization of a war be reexamined annually "after careful scrutiny of the situation by political and military leaders," thus providing either a reaffirmation of commitment or an awareness that conflicting views made sustaining that commitment impracticable.[42] Although officers were not cited as having said so, their observations suggested some distinction between an "Army of the American people" and an Army of the current administration; and the sources for the guidance they offered seemed less the immediate policy of those presently in office than the policy growing from the interests and character of the American people.

The Army's insistence on congressional and popular support as a prerequisite for committing US forces to pursue the administration's policies continued after General Meyer's retirement. In an article in the *Washington Post* on 24 June 1983, Gen John A. Wickham, Jr., the Army chief of staff, was described by his aides as sharing the views of General Meyer concerning the nature of the Central American problems and the strong reasons for not sending US troops there. The same article noted that Lt Gen Robert L. Schweitzer, chairman of the Inter-American Defense Board, was reported as having warned of massive refugee problems for both the United States and Mexico if Central American countries were not protected against "leftist takeovers." Nonetheless, it was deemed possible to be genuinely committed to supporting a given regime without having a major troop deployment to go along with it.[43] Soon after his appointment as Army chief of staff, General Wickham made roughly this same point much more explicitly. Although he refused to disavow the use of US troops in Central America absolutely, he all but did so conditionally. He did not "see the potential for widening of involvement of the American military" in Central America. He declined to intrude on the political leaders' responsibility for judging "the will of the people," but he nonetheless expressed doubt that domestic support existed for sending US troops to Central America; and he considered such support absolutely essential for any deployment to become worthwhile.[44]

Although such views as these had a long and respected—even hallowed— tradition in the United States military, the chronological nearness of the Southeast Asian war probably made it inevitable that some would see them as specific effects of Vietnam. But when General Wickham was asked what impact the Vietnam experience was having on US policies toward Central America, he demurred. "I don't think we should tie ourselves to historical precedent," he told reporters on 8 August 1983. In speaking of "many differences" between Vietnam and Central America, General Wickham pointed to the comparative proximity of Central American nations to the United States, to the changing character of the strategic threat to US interests, and shifts in the "American perception of its role in the world."[45] On the conceptual level, then, where the problems of Vietnam substantially originated, the Army chief disavowed precedents. This meant, however, that Vietnam had no real power over US action in Central America at *any* level, since lesser and more specific decisions can be judged appropriate only with reference to the broader conception.

To be sure, Army officers—both on active duty and retired—were hardly the ones to focus attention on the need for such basic elements of a successful national military enterprise as maintaining popular support and securing a conscious and willing endorsement in Congress. But the frequency with which Army officers avoided stark and simplified references to the presumed impact of Vietnam was unusually high. By contrast, in a speech republished in *Air Force Magazine* in March 1983, retired Air Force Gen T. R. Milton gave a recital of the history of the war in Southeast Asia to present "The Lessons of Vietnam." General Milton described the forces he regarded as key to the failure of US efforts in Vietnam, recognizing that it was crucial for the United States to avoid a knee-jerk reaction. "The very name Vietnam," he said, "has become a code word meaning, to a substantial vocal element in this land of ours, any exercise of military power— however small—in support of national policy." He insisted that pressing problems in the Middle East, Latin America, and the western Pacific demanded that the United States "exorcise the Vietnam ghost if we are ever again to assert ourselves with confidence."[46]

Yet, despite the value one might see in getting the lessons of Vietnam right, it was important to determine who had gotten them wrong. Although "a substantial vocal element" might use the "very name Vietnam" as a code word for military involvements, it was important to know how substantial and how vocal the element was and, perhaps even more, who exactly they were. It was at least an open question who was most haunted by "the Vietnam ghost"; and, ironically but not altogether surprisingly, many military officers and political figures who customarily favored use of such involvements at least in theory were among the most likely to make references to Vietnam. The exorcism for which General Milton called may have been needed as much within the military as in any other significant operating element in the national system.

General Milton himself exemplified this tendency in an article for the *Colorado Springs Sun* on 12 December 1983. A regular contributor of observations and opinion to the newspaper, he began by noting that "there is something disturbingly similar about Lebanon and the early days of Vietnam, much as I hate to invoke that tiresome cliché."[47] What seemed similar to him was excessive caution in "fending off the enemy." Limited responses to hostile fire upon US Marines reminded Milton of the "tit-for-tat" reaction after the Vietcong attacks on B-57 aircraft at Bien Hoa and on the US Army compound at Pleiku. The answer Milton considered appropriate to the riddle of Lebanon was removal of the Marines to ships and launching "a highly visible, and audible, display of air power" as a "demonstration of United States presence."[48] Some aspects of General Milton's recommendation make for some interesting questions in their own right. Was the use of aerial firepower "in a few big air strikes against Syrian batteries in the Bekaa valley" not somehow harking back to the use of military operations as political signals?[49] Could aerial firepower be used profitably as a "demonstration of presence" in a complicated political environment?

The public stance of the highest Army officers, diffident as to the specific pertinence of Vietnam, may have been useful and politic; and it may have also been something of a breastwork behind which the reexamination of experience and some reformulation of doctrine could continue. For even as the Army's highest officers adopted a distinctly pragmatic tone (and as some of their counterparts in sister services openly defended their doctrinally established views in ways that made them sound too much like ideologues), the "worker bees" throughout the armed forces carried the psychic scars of Vietnam.[50] The question was which tone, which approach, and which group would be best poised to seize the moment when the time became ripe for setting out post-Vietnam strategic alternatives in a broad way.

Historical Reflections and a Grasp at the Future

The ultimate practical pay-off of an exercise in historical reflection lies in the coherence and relevance it can bring to one's present and future behavior. The coherence comes if we can grasp a past problem as a whole, gain some sense of the past as having a distinct and integral meaning of its own (even if we misread it), and envision some working relationship between it and our own deep-seated beliefs. Our beliefs need not be "validated" by history in the sense of being proved operationally accurate, but they must be shown to have pertinence. And so reflection is neither name-calling nor an attempt to escape responsibility for one's own failings. The more accurate we sense the reflection to be, the more inclusive of our beliefs and doctrinal interests and past experience it is; and the more extensive over the range of military and security concerns it becomes, the more philosophically satisfying and practically acceptable the interpretation becomes.

A military review of the past may become either a raid on history for verbal plunder with which to decorate one's own self-esteem or a retooling of the self-image. In the aftermath of Vietnam, the Army, more quickly and more effectively than the other US services, took step after step toward this reconstruction. Although there were many variants and versions of strategic thinking within the Army, as elsewhere in the armed forces and in the civilian sector of the defense community, the AirLand Battle concept received the most attention. Advanced as a general approach to warfighting that was not scenario-dependent, the underlying thrust was to reassert maneuver, reaffirm the importance of versatility on the battlefield, and reclaim warfare as a military art and science from those who had treated it largely as political gesture and signal sending and had underplayed the importance of military skills and professionalism.[51] It was inevitable that the Army's doctrinal formulations would touch on the interests and beliefs of the other services.[52] The genius of the Army's concept—soon established as doctrine—was that it took everyone into consideration, although not necessarily in ways that they endorsed, and gave everyone something to do, although not necessarily what they preferred to be doing. It was coherent and comprehensive—and hence relevant and persuasive.

The general spirit of the AirLand Battle concept made it an especially signficant triumph over the installation-heavy US presence in Vietnam. This was hardly to say that the massing of force and the maintenance of suitable supply were not critical; rather, once forces and materiel were massed, the manner in which they manipulated and applied to real military situations was crucial. Masses of troops, ground-force equipment, aircraft, and supplies of all kinds were an especially visible necessity. It was not the "what" that was at issue; it was the "how."

A full statement of the AirLand Battle concept, now emerging as Army doctrine and extending its reach into the thinking of the other services and of other NATO nations, was issued by the US Army Training and Doctrine Command (TRADOC) in 1982. The assignment of responsibilities among services and branches was included, as was a vision of how AirLand Battle would actually function. Refinement continued, but there was little doubt that a serious alternative to defending NATO's eastern frontiers had been posed.[53]

Although the clarity and apparent pertinence of AirLand Battle depended on its response to immediately pressing problems having to do with the relative balance of NATO and Warsaw Pact forces in various categories of units and weapons, its pertinence to the Army drew on a deeper and more complex tradition. In a great many ways, it picked up themes from the late 1950s and very early 1960s that had been either peculiarly transmuted by the events of the Vietnam War or deferred when interest in counterinsurgency ran high. The emphasis on maneuver and on units' abilities to operate for uncertain lengths of time quasi-autonomously was justified in the 1950s as a defense against nuclear attack and as a way of introducing tactical flexibility into even the very high-threat environment of a nuclear war. The centerpiece of the Army's effort to produce this transformation was the "Pentomic Division," advanced most notably by then Chief of Staff Maxwell D. Taylor; and articulations of "nuclear tactics" followed.[54]

General Taylor's emphasis on the nation's need for "flexible response" was soon all but equated with the interest in counterinsurgency and unconventional warfare, but it had really developed with much less departure from the traditional concern over war on the more intense end of the spectrum. The line behind which Taylor wished to stay was "massive retaliation" and all-out war, including strategic nuclear exchange. Tactical nuclear warfare was not only not taboo; thinking about it was imperative if deterrence of anything less than a total nuclear war were to seem credible.[55] The advocates of airmobility within the Army were focused on Europe—on "the big war"—and did not give much thought to the use of helicopters in low-intensity conflicts, counterguerrilla action, and the like.[56] "Flexible response" really meant flexibility in Europe more than it meant anything else, except perhaps for its meaning as a step toward reaffirming the Army's utility in modern warfare and to its right to share in the formulation of military policy.

Such views as appeared in the 1980s, then, had a history themselves. This was modified and molded through time and experience, including that of the Vietnam conflict. Vietnam affected some as an uncomfortable and finally irrelevant distraction, others as an invitation to reexamine the basics of what they were about.

When generalities yielded to policy and budget specifics, the lessons from past experience tended to vary according to service interests and background. In essence, this extended the pattern that had been established during the war. For Lt Gen William W. Dick, Jr., chief of Army research and development, Vietnam demonstrated the need for better armor on helicopters and for an advanced aerial fire support system (AAFSS). Such a helicopter would have twice the speed of those used in Vietnam and would be equipped with improved weapons. The goal was "to satisfy a requirement for an armed air vehicle that can be integrated into US Army maneuver elements to provide commanders with responsive mobile firepower." The AAFSS would be able to operate without an airstrip and under reduced visibility and ceiling, and it would have highly accurate fire control; yet its place in the larger question of interservice competition for post-Vietnam roles could not be overlooked.[57] It clearly posed some measure of competition with aerial support that might be delivered by branches other than the Army.

By contrast, the Marines tended to justify those innovations which they tested in Vietnam as simple outgrowths of their traditional expeditionary role. Apart from the use of helicopters in "vertical assault," Gen Wallace Greene claimed that the full-scale amphibious landing force was again demonstrated as effective and necessary by landings on beachheads in Vietnam. That these landings were unopposed did not bar General Greene from describing them as "a projection of our Nation's seapower ashore." Close air support was proclaimed effective because pilots were doing what they had trained to do—support Marines on the ground; and the logistic support system operated well "because our essential supply system is integrated within our combat units." All was designed, he said, to "relieve the combat marine of all possible administrative burdens while in combat." The expeditionary airfield concept—using aluminum matting spread out over level sand—was described as having been in development for eight years; so the message was that the Marine Corps could be relied on to produce tactics and systems needed for unexpected eventualities. In addition, General Greene praised the Marine air traffic control unit, even at the time when air control was still a knotty issue among the services in Southeast Asia.[58]

In testimony before Congress in 1967, Gen John P. McConnell allowed that the Vietnam experience showed that the Air Force had not given sufficient attention to tactical aviation. "We needed a lot more than we have put into it or have been able to put into it," he said, "particularly in terms of the capability to pinpoint targets at night and in all weather conditions." Similarly, command and control arrangements had not been developed with an eye to appropriate and full coordination with the Army's ground forces.

Nor had ordnance that was suitable for the enemy, the terrain, or the circumstances of delivery been developed. General McConnell believed progress had been achieved in airlift, as well; and overall, he judged that the Air Force had taken to heart some of the key issues raised by the conduct of the war.[59] The differing approaches toward gaining lessons from Vietnam made it possible for the services to pose rival interpretations of the experience there—interpretations that could sustain interservice rivalries.

The effort to short-circuit interservice rivalry between the Army and the Air Force was notable, including development of offices in TRADOC at Fort Monroe, Virginia, and in the headquarters of the Air Force's Tactical Air Command (TAC) at Langley AFB, Virginia, to achieve coordination and resolve potential problems. But these measures, taken to reduce tension and hostility, faced certain troublesome realities. TRADOC was responsible for developing Army doctrine and for seeing to its promulgation. The former task, difficult as it was, led toward definable resolution; but knowing how well the new doctrine was accepted had to be a more elusive matter of estimation. On the other hand, the cooperative achievements in which TAC had a part could not automatically be promulgated throughout the Air Force, since it was largely a horizontally integrated organization. Moreover, a determination to cooperate and to transcend traditional boundaries often runs strong at the very highest ranks while the genuine instincts of the lesser ranking officers and of the troops run contrary. Thus, panels and study groups gave no guarantee that the mechanisms of cooperation would yield a strong and durable product.[60]

Public statements in support of Air Force-Army cooperation appeared in a variety of fora, frequently presented by those whose assignments had put them close to the issue. Typical of such works was an article by Maj James A. Machos, whose "Air-Land Battles or AirLand Battle?" appeared in the July 1983 issue of *Military Review*. Machos referred to AirLand Battle doctrine as a "focus" that emphasized the need for the services to "train and fight together," thereby taking unilateral service initiatives and reaping benefits from their synergism.[61] Adding his own emphasis on the need for swift reaction in the event a war were to break out in Europe, Machos insisted that all tasks be undertaken *"without regard to service rivalry or bias"* (Machos's emphasis).[62] This served, in effect, as an introduction for reevaluating standing Air Force doctrinal views—a comparatively rare public examination of the degree of compatibility between Air Force doctrine and a major Army doctrinal statement that had been construed as having interservice support and agreement. Close-air-support (CAS) doctrine, according to Machos, must be understood to include strikes deeper behind the forward line of own troops (FLOT) than was traditional in CAS thinking. Moreover, he specified that A-10 aircraft (not considered the most glamorous) take a major part in such an effort.[63] Suppression of enemy air defenses (SEAD) had been traditionally regarded as an Air Force counterair mission; Machos noted that "recent developments in air-land battle cooperation" in joint suppression pointed in a different direction, including use of land assets to support tactical air (TACAIR) operations and to free aircraft for roles other than suppression.[64] Machos viewed the traditional definition of interdiction—from the FLOT "to the limits of TACAIR"—as "not sufficient in today's battlefield environment."[65] The notion that interdiction was a TACAIR mission exclusively was "parochial"; Machos advocated a joint responsibility, including the right of ground commanders to "influence interdiction targeting beyond the CAS area of operations."[66] The nature of the war expected in Europe and the vision of the means needed to win it clearly encouraged a rethinking of doctrine.

Col Thomas A. Cardwell III, in a 1984 *Military Review* article, focused on the need to take the generalized agreement on AirLand Battle as a concept and to implement it with practical steps. He specified that these were necessary to ensure that genuine agreement on command and control would be in place well before any combat action was undertaken. Cardwell concluded that much of the writing and discussion that had taken place on AirLand Battle was "simply a rehash of Army thinking that had been kicking around for the past 40 years."[67] Reevaluation was driven by the Army's expansion of the geographical area included within its scope of influence and interest.[68] Cardwell was enthusiastic about the Army-Air Force cooperation in developing a joint operational concept for attack of the "second echelon" (J-SAK, published on 13 December 1982), the only basis for full resolution of any differences of view and an approach that was to "come to grips with the control issue."[69] Acting as if the problems were essentially technical could not solve the basic problems; even within the armed forces, let alone in the services' relations with civilian leaders, the seemingly technical and operational question was a political one.

Still, a long history lay behind each service's special positions. Each carried deeply held views on how to deter or fight a war most effectively, and organizational biases and interests emerged in support of those variant "ways of war."[70] Ingrained dispositions did not die easily. A mid-1983 report called the Air Force "a reluctant partner in the new Army strategy"; it was "paying lip service" to AirLand Battle. In an article in the 18 June 1983 issue of *National Journal*, Michael R. Gordon noted that there was considerable positive comment on the Army's return to "tactical literacy" and that the doctrine in general had a good reception in Congress, among defense analysts, in the defense industry, and in the press.[71] Apart from the worries of some Europeans that the emphasis on tactical flexibility in AirLand Battle meant advancing into Warsaw Pact territory, the key difficulties lay in turning the generality into the specifics of missions and resources.

Recognizing an eagerness to turn away from reliance on firepower as the key to tactical success, Gordon quoted a study done at Fort Leavenworth by Maj Robert A. Doughty on "The Evolution of US Army Tactical Doctrine, 1946-1976." Doughty noted that, in the past, "maneuver was used primarily for locating and fixing the enemy."[72]

Observations drawn largely from the Arab-Israeli War of 1973, which showed the startling capabilities of antitank weapons, cast doubt on extreme reliance on firepower; and a growing apprehension of the mass of armor available to the Warsaw Pact added to the need for reexamination. Although the 1976 version of Army Field Manual (FM) 100-5, *Operations*, still talked in terms of needing a 6-1 ratio of superiority to conduct an offensive counterattack, it also recognized the situation facing the Army as "unprecedented." Maintaining advantageous force ratios along potentially threatened fronts by massing troops tends to suggest fixed positions, inadequate flexible reserves, and the taking of enemy echelons in succession.[73] Viewed closely, there were serious differences among various Army tactical doctrines proposed during the 1970s; yet, seen from a greater distance, they formed a trend toward enhanced flexibility of the ground forces. While firepower remained critical, it was not controlling—it was necessary to have it, but it was equally necessary that it not govern the way in which forces were disposed or how they were employed. This formed the basis for potential difficulties with the Air Force, since the Army's enhanced maneuver suggested—at least to them—the need for greater control over firepower assets, including aircraft. Assuming the primacy of ground force maneuverability as the determinant of tactical operations, it is hardly surprising that ground commanders would want a say in where their support was coming from. Against this grasp was the Air Force's interest in air superiority and in suppressing enemy air defenses. The question to be resolved was the balance between goals that called for autonomous operations and those in which closely coordinated joint action was imperative. The answer was not immediately clear.

That there was some reluctance and sense of reservation within the Army itself did become clear—not necessarily to oppose AirLand Battle as such but to puzzle over the wars of greatest likelihood and to determine how best to prepare for future contingencies. Since the ascent of AirLand Battle came as a reciprocal of the decline of theory and practice in counterinsurgency, those who were concerned about retaining capabilities in the low-intensity end of the spectrum of conflict had some basis for their worries. Perhaps the commitment to maneuver by larger, well-trained, more heavily equipped units in a theater such as Central Europe meant a desertion of other possible levels of commitment.[74] In a sharp critique of the Army and its attitude toward counterinsurgency operations delivered at a meeting of the International Studies Association in March 1984, West Point instructor Andrew F. Krepinevich, Jr., quoted Lt Gen William P. Yarborough, former commander of the Special Warfare Center: "We didn't cope with irregular warfare in Asia; therefore we've closed the door on it and, rather than recognizing that we didn't learn our lessons, we are turning back again in the hope that there will be a conventional war if there is a war and we'll use our conventional forces...."[75] Krepinevich disputed the claims that the 1st Special Operations Command (SOCOM) established in October 1982 at Fort Bragg, North Carolina, really could meet the demands of counterinsurgency action. He concluded that SOCOM's units "far better suited for the execution of economy of force operations in support of main force Army units conducting conventional operations."[76] General Yarborough, for his part, believed that high-ranking Army officers really thought of special operations forces merely as commandos.[77] Further, Krepinevich saw the talk of lightness and swiftness of response of the Central Command (CENTCOM) as garbled by the inclusion of a "dual-hat" responsibility to speak to counterinsurgency contingencies. The historic problem was that "dual hatting" usually meant that one role or the other would take second place and then take successive hits to its force structure and other requirements. In short, some of the questioners acknowledged that change was taking place; but they were less certain that it constituted progress—less certain that it was likely to meet the real future needs of the service and of the country.

Emphasis on maneuver appeared in Marine publications as well; and there, too, concern developed that the appearance of novelty and the thrust for a persuasive new doctrine would soon be running square into the realities of a contrary form of warfare. Writing in *Marine Corps Gazette* in July 1983, Michael P. Palladino urged that Marines remember "another kind of war" such as that fought in Vietnam, asserting that "the irregular soldier has become the warrior of the late 20th century."[78] Palladino believed that the lessons of Vietnam were "forgotten before they were assimilated or applied"; and he warned of "myopia when training ... Marines." Highly motivated and sensitized to the possibilities of nuclear, biological, and chemical warfare, the Marine was nonetheless unskilled in other ways. "What," Palladino asked, "does he do when he is called to hump through the jungles of El Salvador chasing an elusive foe?" The problem was that training did not encompass the range of likely wars. "Preparing Marines to fight conventional, mobile operations in the Delta corridor at Twentynine Palms is not preparation for the most likely contingency," Palladino added. "A Marine's physical readiness is constantly stressed; however, his psychological conditioning is sadly ignored." And focusing attention and training effort on what Palladino saw as less likely forms of warfare, the Marines strengthened their chances of "reinventing the wheel" if they were actually committed to low-intensity conflicts. "Counterinsurgency and antiterrorist techniques should be second nature," he said, "not a new experience."[79] Yet Patrick L. Townsend, a retired Marine major and businessman, raised some question as to the likely pace at which Marines would accept such advice as Palladino's. Writing in *Newsweek* on 30 January 1984, Townsend spoke of the Corps' persistent bias in favor of chivalry, its belief in fighting by the same set of rules, and its incomprehension of intentionally suicidal behavior (as distinct from improvisational self-sacrifice) as magnificent but perhaps "outdated."[80] Clearly, however, the reluctance to train in a fashion that either Townsend or Palladino thought necessary did not stem from a lack of zeal. It grew from a different way of looking at the world of warriors and from a different sense of the prevailing rules of war.[81]

Despite the difficulties inevitably facing the services as they sought to build the necessary forces and doctrines to meet the nation's security objectives, expressions of hope periodically arose that such problems would be overcome when emergency became clear. In peacetime, when the services were traditionally focusing on the strengthening of their own resources, professions of cooperation were not always accompanied by agreement on how best to share either the budget or mission responsibilities. At the very highest military levels, recognition of the high priority to be attached to cooperation was often extremely keen. Yet the enthusiasm below that level or at high rank outside the professional military was often well below fever pitch, until it reached those actually charged with direct combat responsibility.

What concrete measures would ensure that periods rich with professions of cooperative spirit did not wither into cycles of disappointment and frustration? It may have been a modest sign of hope that discussions on unity of command in emergencies could take place at high levels, but what lessons were being absorbed into the functional routines, expectations, and inclinations of the troops at large? The historical record provided little reason to believe that peacetime differences would be suspended or resolved in war. Dwight Eisenhower, while serving as the key military adviser to President Truman during the era of post-World War II military reorganization, provided exactly such an assurance, noting that everything got ironed out once the flag of war went up. His own experience in World War II should have told him better; and later experience clearly contradicted Eisenhower. Not alone, but surely notable, was the case of the Vietnam War, in which provisions on command and control and other issues that had thrived on paper before the mid-1960s were supplanted by "adhocracy."

Strategy and tactics that win the largest attention in peacetime ought to show up in improved performance in wartime; and there is little reason to expect that an actual war would escape the impact of peacetime shortcomings. In any given time, however, the persuasiveness of strategic formulation and tactical doctrine depends on coherence and apparent relevance. Yet such persuasiveness can itself be seductive; and added attention to the underlying implications of such strategic and tactical ideas is critical. In the case of AirLand Battle, for example, the attractiveness of coherence is counterbalanced by differences of view. Ground-force thinkers are interested in some measure of decentralization in control, notwithstanding enhancements in communications technology, while some in the Air Force are concerned about the possible fragmentation of air power. And what if this vision of present interests through analysis of the past proves inaccurate, despite its eminent coherence? A "new Vietnam" would not be found in superficial features of jungle terrain but in the confusion and indecision that follows the deterioration of peacetime certitudes.

Notes

1. Carl Becker, *Every Man His Own Historian* (New York: F. S. Crofts and Co., 1935). The dialogue between the historical event and the later observer bears some similarity to the interaction of a user and an immense data base. The data cannot speak for themselves but are structured into some semblance of meaning by the user's choices. The seemingly endless recombinations into which the data may be formed reflect the interests, biases, and present knowledge of that user. It remains, in some measure, a "bootstrap" experience in which the direction of the user's learning is potentially restricted or at least framed by assumptions.

2. The literature on the American Civil War is, simply, vast. Useful tools for exploring the literature of the American Civil War are Robin Higham, ed., *A Guide to the Sources of U.S. Military History* (Hamden, Conn.: Archon Books, 1975); and Robin Higham and Donald J. Mrozek, *A Guide to the Sources of the U.S. Military History, Supplement I* (Hamden, Conn.: Archon Books, 1981).

3. An excellent study of the debate during the post-Civil War era may be found in Russell F. Weigley, *Towards an American Army* (New York: Columbia University Press, 1962). The argument was carried on, notably, by high-level officials such as John A. Logan, a United States senator and political boss of Illinois as well as the Republican candidate for vice president in 1884. A major general of volunteers in the Civil War, Logan wrote a lengthy book titled *The Volunteer Soldier of America* (Chicago: R. S. Peale, 1887) in which he defended the militia on the basis of Civil War experience. Opposing Logan was former professor of natural philosophy at Washington University in St. Louis, major general in the regular Army, and secretary of war after Edwin Stanton, John M. Schofield. Schofield, *Forty-six Years in the Army* (New York: Century Co., 1897).

4. The classic example of reinterpretation of southern institutions at the start of the twentieth century is U. B. Phillips, *Life and Labor in the Old South* (Boston: Little, Brown and Co., 1929).

5. Concerning the Franco-Prussian War and its impact on French thinking about the nature of warfighting, see Michael Howard, *The Franco-Prussian War: The German Invasion of France 1870-1871* (New York: Macmillan, 1961); and Barbara Tuchman, *The Guns of August* (New York: Macmillan, 1962).

6. On the sharply differing ways in which World War I and its origins were assessed, see, for example, Sidney B. Fay, *The Origins of the World War* (New York: Macmillan Co., 1928); and Harry Elmer Barnes, *The Genesis of the World War* (New York: A. A. Knopf, 1929).

7. Paul Hendrickson, "McNamara: Specters of Vietnam," *Washington Post*, 10 May 1984, B-1.

8. Ibid.

9. It is somewhat intriguing that the various armed forces, which traditionally call attention to what they see as externally based threats to US security and use it to justify rallying in

common policy, are affected by a sense of threat to their own particular doctrine. This appears to encourage a "closing of ranks" to protect their doctrine, even as the closing ranks in the larger scene is to protect the commander in chief. On the doctrinal matter, however, the process can easily lead to a firming of the differences between the services rather than to an enhancement of their common ground.

10. The quoted term comes from Richard Hofstadter's description of John C. Calhoun's process of mind. Richard Hofstadter, *The American Political Tradition and the Men Who Made It* (New York: A. A. Knopf, 1948).

11. Among the guides for entering the massive literature on the Vietnam War are Joe P. Dunn, "In Search of Lessons: The Development of a Vietnam Historiography," *Parameters* 9, no. 4 (1979); and Peter Braestrup, ed., *Vietnam as History, Ten Years After the Paris Peace Accords* (Washington, D.C.: University Press of America, 1984).

Among the works in the Vietnam Studies series are James L. Collins, Jr., *The Development and Training of the South Vietnamese Army, 1950-1972* (Washington, D.C.: Department of the Army, 1975); George S. Eckhardt, *Command and Control, 1950-1969* (Washington, D.C.: Department of the Army, 1974); Julian J. Ewell and Ira A. Hunt, Jr., *Sharpening the Combat Edge: The Use of Analysis to Reinforce Military Judgment* (Washington, D.C.: Department of the Army, 1974); William B. Fulton, *Riverine Operations, 1966-1969* (Washington, D.C.: Department of the Army, 1973); John H. Hay, Jr., *Tactical and Materiel Innovations* (Washington, D.C.: Department of the Army, 1974); Joseph M. Heiser, Jr., *Logistic Support* (Washington, D.C.: Department of the Army, 1974); Stanley Robert Larsen and James Lawton Collins, Jr., *Allied Participation in Vietnam* (Washington, D.C.: Department of the Army, 1975); Joseph A. McChristian, *The Role of Military Intelligence, 1965-1967* (Washington, D.C.: Department of the Army, 1974); Charles R. Myer, *Division-level Communications, 1962-1973* (Washington, D.C.: Department of the Army, 1982); Spurgeon Neal, *Medical Support of the U.S. Army in Vietnam, 1965-1970* (Washington, D.C.: Department of the Army, 1975); David Ewing Ott, *Field Artillery, 1954-1973* (Washington, D.C.: Department of the Army, 1975); Robert R. Ploger, *U.S. Army Engineers, 1965-1970* (Washington, D.C.: Department of the Army, 1974); and Leonard B. Taylor, *Financial Management of the Vietnam Conflict, 1962-1972* (Washington, D.C.: Department of the Army, 1974).

Typical of the works produced in Indochina Monographs are Hoang Ngoc Lung, *Strategy and Tactics* (Washington, D.C.: US Army Center of Military History, 1980); Cao Van Vien et al., *The U.S. Adviser* (Washington, D.C.: US Army Center of Military History, 1980); and Soutchay Vongsavanh, *RLG Military Operations and Activities in the Laotian Panhandle* (Washington, D.C.: US Army Center of Military History, 1981).

12. Fulton and Neal.

13. Donn A. Starry, *Armored Combat in Vietnam* (Indianapolis: Bobbs-Merrill Co. Inc., 1980).

14. Bernard C. Rogers, *Cedar Falls-Junction City, A Turning Point* (Washington, D.C.: Department of the Army, 1974).

15. Dave Richard Palmer, *Summons of the Trumpet* (San Rafael, Calif.: Presidio Press, 1978), xix.

16. Harry G. Summers, Jr., *On Strategy: The Vietnam War in Context* (Carlisle Barracks, Pa.: Strategic Studies Institute, US Army War College, 1981). Emblematic of the wide currency given to Summers's arguments concerning Vietnam is "Man of the Hour," *Parade* magazine, 14 August 1983, 9, in which a capsule biography on Summers is coupled with a short description of his views and reference to the compatibility of *On Strategy* with the thinking of Gen John Vessey, Jr., chairman of the Joint Chiefs of Staff.

17. "Man of the Hour," 9.

18. An interesting illustration of the acceptability of Summers's work outside the Army was its circulation to all members of the Air War College class of 1983 and to the War College's faculty. In the particular circumstances of its circulation, the book was clearly meant not only

as an aid to appreciating the underlying principles of war in contemporary conflict and to making sense out of a reading of Clausewitz's own works on war but also as a substantial, if not total, endorsement of Summers's understanding of Vietnam. The assertion of a single, central authority over the opposing side in that war was certainly convenient and comfortable for a service that traditionally boosted the importance of centralized control and whose specific weapons and tactical and strategic doctrine militated in favor of "war against the source" of the problem—in this case, Hanoi and the sinews of its warmaking capability. What was thus, in effect, a "big war" interpretation of the Vietnam conflict, as well as a simplified one, may actually have been not only tolerable in many Air Force audiences, but especially welcome. There remained, however, the further question of what underlying assumptions were being accepted along with the surface support for conventional air power propositions. In keeping the baby, perhaps they would also get stuck with the bathwater.

19. It is more supportable to argue that failing to see the extent of genuine, indigenous hostility to the Diem regime in Saigon and its successors was far closer to the actual problem. Even when accepting that the problems in the South were largely Saigon's responsibility and that inability to remedy manifest defects was the enduring source of danger, US officials at the highest levels observed that North Vietnamese involvement was the sine qua non for guaranteeing that fighting would continue, that it might escalate, and that a mood of unrest and instability could stand firmly against all of Washington's hopes and Saigon's professionals.

20. Extensive material on the subject may be found in the various collections in the John F. Kennedy and Lyndon B. Johnson Presidential Libraries. See, for example, Walt Rostow, speech, US Army Special Warfare School, Fort Bragg, N.C., 28 June 1961; Army 1961 folder, Departments and Agencies Files, President's Office Files, Papers of John F. Kennedy, Kennedy Library.

21. It is also worth wondering exactly what Johnson would have needed to do to gain popular support for an enhanced war effort, presumably at the expense of domestic social programs. The mixture of optimism and criticism in American society during the 1960s meshed with growing anger and anguish over the Vietnam War; but they preceded the emergence of the war as the consummate public issue of the day. Moreover, the "quick-and-dirty" operation in the Dominican Republic in 1965 played to mixed reviews, even though it was not complicated by significant resistance even from those Dominicans hostile to the US intervention. The criticism of Johnson for seeking to have it both ways on Vietnam and the Great Society has some merit; what it lacks is an alternative that encompasses both tracks, each of which Johnson perceived as a proper and even necessary course.

22. Civilian writers such as Stephen Peter Rosen touch on some of these issues, as does Summers. Also see Harry G. Summers, Jr., "Defense without Purpose," *Transaction/Social Science and Modern Society* 21, no. 1 (November–December 1983): 4–33.

23. Specific expectations of what sort of war was possible and what sort of military conduct best suited the American temperament could lead, through a long train of logic, to continued emphasis on technological substitutes for manpower and many other traditional themes. If one put it cynically, one might argue that it was the logic necessary to explain concentration on strategic forces, on the rebuilding of main conventional forces, and on the enhancement of various weapon systems for high-value areas such as Germany, as with improved attack helicopters.

24. Summers, *On Strategy*.

25. Ibid.

26. Drew Middleton, "U.S. Generals Are Leery of Latin Intervention," *New York Times*, 21 June 1983. Among those specifically mentioned were Gen John W. Vessey, Jr., chairman of the Joint Chiefs of Staff, and Gen Edward C. Meyer, then Army chief of staff.

27. Donn A. Starry, *Mounted Combat in Vietnam* (Washington, D.C.: Department of the Army, 1978), subsequently released commercially as *Armored Combat in Vietnam* in nearly

identical form. Also see William W. Momyer, *Air Power in Three Wars*, ed. A. J. C. Lavalle and James C. Gaston (n.p., n.d.).

28. Starry.

29. Harry G. Summers, Jr., "Alabama and Vietnam," *Montgomery Advertiser-Journal*, 23 October 1983.

30. Frank Futrell et al., *Aces & Aerial Victories: The United States Air Force in Southeast Asia, 1965-1973*, ed. James N. Eastman, Jr., Walter Hanak, and Lawrence J. Paszek (Washington, D.C.: Office of Air Force History, 1976); and John Albright, John A. Cash, and Allan W. Sandstrum, *Seven Firefights in Vietnam* (Washington, D.C.: US Army Office of the Chief of Military History, 1970).

31. Bernard C. Nalty, *Air Power and the Fight for Khe Sanh* (Washington, D.C.: Office of Air Force History, 1973); and Moyers S. Shore II, *The Battle for Khe Sanh* (Washington, D.C.: Historical Branch, US Marine Corps, 1969).

32. Edwin Brickford Hooper, Dean C. Allard, and Oscar P. Fitzgerald, *The United States Navy in the Vietnam Conflict*, vol. 1, *The Setting of the Stage to 1959* (Washington, D.C.: Department of the Navy, 1976); Jack Shulimson, *U.S. Marines in Vietnam, 1966: An Expanding War* (Washington, D.C.: History and Museums Division, Headquarters US Marine Corps, 1982); Robert F. Futrell, *The Advisory Years to 1965* (Washington, D.C.: Office of Air Force History, 1981). It is inconclusive but suggestive that the Futrell manuscript was revised to focus more narrowly on South Vietnam instead of dealing with activities during the advisory years on a more integrative basis throughout Southeast Asia, while Shulimson revealed the degree to which the Marines regarded the indigenous antigovernment forces in South Vietnam as a real "player" in the war even after the introduction of main force combat units of the North Vietnamese Army (NVA).

33. Jack S. Ballard, *Development and Employment of Fixed-Wing Gunships 1962-1972* (Washington, D.C.: Office of Air Force History, 1982); William A. Buckingham, Jr., *Operation Ranch Hand: The Air Force and Herbicides in Southeast Asia 1961-1971* (Washington, D.C.: Office of Air Force History, 1982).

34. Momyer; and U. S. Grant Sharp, *Strategy for Defeat, Vietnam in Retrospect* (San Rafael, Calif.: Presidio Press, 1978).

35. Although Momyer is open for some challenge and perhaps criticism for what seems a single-minded devotion to a quite conservative vision of air power and a somewhat confined version of wars suited to American characteristics and resources, he cannot be similarly faulted for his lack of enthusiasm for limited war *theories*. Perhaps less grief would have been caused had the wealth of historical *practice* in limited war been given even half the attention lavished on *theory*.

36. Specialized works from certain Air Force sources laid claim to respect for their professional achievements, while avoiding the pit of mere self-flattery. See, for example, Charles K. Hopkins, *SAC Tanker Operations in the Southeast Asia War* (Offutt AFB, Nebr.: Office of the Historian, Headquarters Strategic Air Command, 1979). At roughly the same time, however, a few works began to appear which, while acknowledging the achievements of Air Force and other service personnel, implicitly accepted that learning from the events of the war could well require going beyond serving as a cheering section to providing a measure of constructive criticism. See, for example, Alan L. Gropman, *Airpower and the Evacuation of Kham Duc* (Maxwell AFB, Ala.: Airpower Research Institute, 1979); and, especially, John J. Lane, Jr., *Command and Control and Communications Structures in Southeast Asia* (Maxwell AFB, Ala.: Airpower Research Institute, 1981). Still, such works concentrated on what air power assets could do, how they could be employed effectively, and what structures were needed to use them purposefully and efficiently. The comprehensive principles of war abided in the background, perhaps; but they did so largely as guides to assessing air power and its applications more than as ways of understanding air power's broader place in interactive relationship with

other forms of military power and other services' management of segments of that overall power.

37. Sharp.
38. Drew Middleton, "Vietnam and the Military Mind," *New York Times Magazine*, 10 January 1982.
39. Ibid.
40. Ibid.
41. Middleton, "U.S. Generals Are Leery of Latin Intervention." Ironically, such measures also had attracted favorable interest from such opponents of the Vietnam War as Senator J. William Fulbright.
42. Ibid.
43. George C. Wilson, "Top U.S. Brass Wary on Central America," *Washington Post*, 24 June 1983.
44. "Army chief assures limited role for U.S.," *Washington Times*, 9 August 1983.
45. Ibid.
46. T. R. Milton, "The Lessons of Vietnam," *Air Force Magazine*, March 1983, 106.
47. T. R. Milton, "Don't Let the Marines Be Sitting Ducks," *Colorado Springs Sun*, 12 December 1983, 20.
48. Ibid.
49. Ibid.
50. Richard Halloran, "For Military Leaders, the Shadow of Vietnam," *New York Times Magazine*, 20 March 1984, 12.
51. The literature on AirLand Battle is considerable; these are only a sampling of expositions and commentaries on the subject: US Army Training and Doctrine Command, "AirLand Battle 2000," 4 September 1981, Fort Monroe, Va.; US Army Training and Doctrine Command, "AirLand Battle 2000," 10 August 1982, Fort Monroe, Va.; US Army Science Board, *Report of Panel on the Future Development Goal* (Washington, D.C.: Department of the Army, 1983); Lt Gen William R. Richardson, "Training for Maneuver Warfare," *Armor* 90 (July–August 1981): 31–34; Phillip A. Karber, "The Growing Armor/Anti Armor Imbalance in Central Europe," *Armed Forces Journal International* 118 (July 1981): 37–40; Defense Nuclear Agency, "Analysis of Some Alternative Tactical Nuclear Doctrines for the US/NATO Corps in the Airland Battle" (Washington, D.C.: 1 December 1981); William G. Hanne, "Airland Battle and the Operational Maneuver Group" (Carlisle Barracks, Pa.: US Army Strategic Studies Institute, 16 May 1983); David Hamilton, "Close Air Support and Battlefield Air Interdiction in the AirLand Battle" (Fort Leavenworth, Kans.: May 1983); Roderick J. Isler, "The Airland Battle—Command, Control and Communications Countermeasures (C^3CM) Integration," Research Report (Maxwell AFB, Ala.: Air Command and Staff College, March 1982); Joseph R. Redden, "Airland Battle—the Global Doctrine?" (Carlisle Barracks, Pa.: US Army War College, 1983); "AirLand Battle Doctrine," Art of War Colloquium (Carlisle Barracks, Pa.: US Army War College, June 1983); John R. Landry et al., "Strategic and Doctrinal Implications of Deep Attack Concepts for the Defense of Europe" (Washington, D.C.: National War College, April 1983).
52. Again, given the different characteristics of the several services, the interplay between the Army and the Air Force inevitably had to be major—perhaps more so than between the Army and the Navy and Marines—because of the need to allocate responsibility in such matters as close air support and interdiction. Just to define such terms, let alone establish patterns of command and control, was to enter a bothersomely sensitive border area where the missions and aspirations of the services sometimes seemed to overlap.
53. "AirLand Battle 2000."
54. Maxwell D. Taylor, *The Uncertain Trumpet* (New York: Harper, 1960); Theodore C. Mataxis and Seymour L. Goldberg, *Nuclear Tactics, Weapons, and Firepower in the Pentomic Division, Battle Group, and Company* (Harrisburg, Pa.: Military Service Publishing Co., 1958).

55. Henry A. Kissinger, *Nuclear Weapons and Foreign Policy* (New York: Harper, 1957).

56. See the numerous oral history interviews in the "History of Army Aviation Series" prepared by the US Army Military History Research Institute, Carlisle Barracks, Pa.

57. Testimony of Lt Gen William W. Dick, Jr., in Senate, Committee on Armed Services and Subcommittee of the Committee on Appropriations, *Hearings on Military Procurement Authorizations for Fiscal Year 1967*, 89th Cong., 2d sess., 10 March 1966, 555–56, 558, 563, 564.

58. Testimony of Gen Wallace M. Greene, Jr., in Senate, Committee on Armed Services and Subcommittee of the Committee on Appropriations, *Hearings on Military Procurement Authorizations for Fiscal Year 1967*, 89th Cong., 2d sess., 24 March 1966, 671–73.

59. Testimony of Gen John P. McConnell in Senate, Committee on Armed Services and Subcommittee of the Committee on Appropriations, *Hearings on Military Procurement Authorizations for Fiscal Year 1968*, 90th Cong., 1st sess., 2 February 1967, 897.

60. Some observers have orally considered the thought that TAC's willingness to be cooperative in the Air Force "interface" with AirLand Battle was related to the compatibility between a preference in TAC for substantially autonomous operation and the Army's desire to have more influence over targeting and mission execution as the area of contact with the enemy came closer to areas of interest to ground forces. The compatibility stemmed in part from what TAC would be willing to "get rid of," less as a matter of concession for the sake of cooperation than from a lack of interest and commitment to certain nonautonomous missions. It also stemmed in part from the Army's willingness to cover some of its own aerial firepower requirements and, some hinted, from the Army's eagerness to press forward with its new helicopters and perhaps moderately larger fixed-wing aircraft.

61. James A. Machos, "Air-Land Battles or AirLand Battle?" *Military Review* 63, no. 7 (July 1983): 33–40. Machos was also a graduate of the US Army Command and General Staff College, and he had been an exchange officer with the Luftwaffe; he also served with the 474th Tactical Fighter Wing at Nellis AFB, Nev.

62. Ibid., 34.

63. Ibid., 36.

64. Ibid., 36–37.

65. Ibid., 37.

66. Ibid., 38–39.

67. Col Thomas A. Cardwell III, USAF, "One Step Beyond—AirLand Battle, Doctrine not Dogma," *Military Review* 64, no. 4 (April 1984): 46.

68. Ibid., 48.

69. Ibid.

70. The concept of "way of war" is central to Russell F. Weigley, *The American Way of War* (New York: Macmillan, 1973). The concept might serve as a useful analytical device for suggesting the way in which deep-seated attitudes have undergirded the more visible arguments over budgetary and other matters.

71. Michael R. Gordon, "The Army's Air-Land Battle Doctrine Worries Allies, Upsets the Air Force," *National Journal*, 18 June 1983, 1274–77.

72. Ibid., 1274.

73. Ibid., 1275.

74. The term *more heavily equipped*, which would seem to contradict the Army's development of light divisions in the 1980s, is not intended in such a contradicting way but only as a description of size and armament relative to counterinsurgency forces.

75. Andrew F. Krepinevich, Jr., "The Army Counterinsurgency Operations: 'Plus Ça Change . . .'" (Paper delivered at the 25th annual meeting of the International Studies Association, 27–31 March 1984, Atlanta, Ga.), 9.

76. Ibid., 10–11.

77. Ibid., 9.

78. Michael P. Palladino, "Remembering Another Kind of War," *Marine Corps Gazette*, July 1983. Also see M. D. Wyly, "War without Firepower?" *Marine Corps Gazette* 67, no. 3 (March 1983): 17–18.

79. Ibid.

80. Patrick L. Townsend, "The Marines' Weak Spot," *Newsweek*, 30 January 1984.

81. In a sense, the term *rules of war* is somewhat deceptive; Townsend and others would surely not suggest that an agreed code of conduct in war even existed. What had happened, rather, was that traditional standards—those developed over time among military professionals as a matter of gradually accepted custom—had been abruptly impeached by ardent fighters whose standards differed in essential ways. In such an environment, testing one's individual conduct against a known general code is likely to be threatened—perhaps supplanted—by the mere observation of the actual conduct of one's various opponents so as to establish a relevant protective attitude and habit.

CHAPTER 3

INTERPRETING VIETNAM: SCHOOL SOLUTIONS

An important vehicle through which the Air Force and the other services express their view of the world around them and their sense of the future is a system of professional military education. This system includes, most notably, the established schools that serve to train, indoctrinate, and, less often, educate officers in those areas deemed important by the faculties of the institutions and their supervising authorities. What is included within the curriculum of a given school does not necessarily indicate precisely what a service thinks, but it is a clue to what is on the minds of many within that service—a certification of things worth thinking about. In this sense, how a curriculum is structured indicates what "really matters" to a service—what is supposed to be crucial to the officers at the level of rank targeted by the given school. The various curricula of the several schools—ranging from squadron level through staff school to war college for Air Force officers—provide some hint of what sort of war is envisioned as the most serious, most likely, or most suited to a service's capabilities.

How the services constructed educational and training programs for officers in the later years of the Vietnam War and after the defeat of the Saigon regime helps to explain how certain lacunae—missing elements—appeared in the military's interpretation of the Vietnam experience. Each service had its own angle of entry into explaining what happened in Vietnam, partly because a key problem for any observer was not just what happened in Southeast Asia generally but what happened to one's own service while it was deployed there. Thus, inevitably, the special historical development and tradition of each service tended to condition the kind of experience it had in Vietnam. Although the services approached handling the Vietnam experience in somewhat different ways, they handled it with similar tools. One such tool was the apparatus of professional military education.

Learning at Leavenworth

Perhaps no school in the professional military education system may be regarded as "typical." The US Army Command and General Staff College, however, can surely be regarded as having significantly reflected the trends and pressures that affected all military schools after Vietnam. Unlike some members of other services who had served in Southeast Asia without having been stationed in South Vietnam (indeed, some of them never set foot on Vietnamese soil), Army officers often had close associations with Vietnamese officers. Deep and positive feelings for the land in which they fought were not uncommon. The personal stakes of the war were high—painfully so as US efforts came to naught with the collapse of the Saigon regime in 1975. One can only speculate as to whether the sense of loss was greater in one service or another and whether that sense contributed to a desire to come to grips with what had happened or to enter a period of denial and avoidance. What did seem to emerge at Leavenworth was an underlying taste for a clear and uncompromised message. If the Army was in need of rebuilding, let there be no confusion as to the architecture of its future. Whether the Army could learn from Vietnam presupposed that it had some sense of what had happened there—some reasonably coherent vision that provided a common ground from which to mine lessons for future operations. In the face of uncertainties about Vietnam itself and in a period when the ongoing war presented knotty political problems for the military, it is not surprising that such a common ground proved difficult to identify. Instead, in 1972–73, the 38-week course of the US Army Command and General Staff College (CGSC) was dominated by scenarios derived from the NATO region and from concentration on staff skills and procedures. Vietnam was explicitly included in only a very few of the 1,430 academic hours that comprised the total course.[1] (The most prominent hypothetical case of insurgency was placed in Venezuela.) *Limited war* was defined in terms of Korea; and, despite its critical importance to Israel's survival, the Arab-Israeli War of 1967 was used as an additional limited war case study. Low-intensity conflict slipped below the attention of the course and curriculum designers, due in part to the perceived need to familiarize students with operations and staff work at corps and army levels. Although this emphasis can be praised as transcending mere pressures of the moment, it also represented an incipient interpretation of Vietnam as essentially a conventional war. At the same time, CGSC saw Vietnam as largely a "botched job," "not much of a war," and no worthy source of lessons for the future. Specific course topics and themes sharpened this leaning toward war "beyond the jungles." The rhetoric and dynamics of counterinsurgency fell on even harder times.[2]

"Special weapons" remained the code for nuclear, biological, and chemical (NBC) weapons; and the purpose of discussing them was to promote "defensive planning of a mechanized division."[3] Also, although the description of the course in tactics, "principles and doctrine pertaining to . . . tactical employment of Army divisions (except airborne)," was suited to the mission of the school and the rank of its students, it actually reinforced

TABLE 1

Case Studies Used in CGSC Courses, 1972–73
Geographic Location of Scenario

Course	Subject	Hours
1. Staff Operations	USA	11
	General or not scenario-dependent	6
	NATO or fictitious European setting	5
2. Leadership and Management	USA	4
	General or not scenario-dependent	4
	Fictitious European	1
	Southeast Asia	1
3. Tactics	General fictitious setting	6
	NATO (Germany or other)	5
	USA	4
	General or not scenario-dependent	3
	Republic of South Africa	2
	Warsaw Pact	2
	Yugoslavia	2
	Korea	1
4. Logistics	General or fictitious	4
	Balkans	1
	Spain	1
5. Strategic Studies	General or not scenario-dependent	8
	USA	8
	USSR	3
	PRC	2
	India	2
	Cambodia	1
	Eastern Europe	1
	Far East	1
	Italy	1
	Japan	1
	Middle East	1
	Republic of South Africa	1

TABLE 1—continued

Course	Subject	Hours
6. Joint and Combined Operations	NATO	4
	Fictitious European	3
	USA	2
	General or not scenario-dependent	1
	Korea	1
	Morocco	1
7. Security Assistance	General or fictitious	6
	Venezuela	2
	Malaya	1
	USA	1
8. General Subjects	General or not scenario-dependent	14
	Fictitious Asia	1
	Brazil	1
	Canada	1
	France	
	Germany	1
	Great Britain	1
	Japan	1
	North Atlantic	1
		1

Source: Based on Program of Instruction (POI), 1972–73, CGSC (rev. 15 September 1972).

the vision of a proper and perhaps preferred war as one that differed manifestly from the enterprise in Southeast Asia.[4] When Southeast Asia appeared in the curriculum, it was more likely to do so as a locus of administrative issues than of combat lessons. In the course on Leadership and Management (Course 2), for example, Southeast Asia was mined for examples of how drug abuse and racial tensions constituted environmental factors at all levels of command.[5] On the basis of actual experience, comparable illustrations could easily have been taken from NATO settings. One can only wonder whether the decision to use Vietnam as the example of poor discipline affected perceptions of the war itself.

The largest course-unit comprehensively devoted to issues related to insurgency and low-intensity conflict dealt with security assistance and its validation within the curriculum derived from its supporting CGSC's mission to prepare officers "as Military Assistance Advisors (less language and area orientation)."[6] In essence, security assistance issues were construed generically; and the principal methods for handling local and regional problems remained those with seemingly worldwide applicability, even though familiarity with local context was essential for the most effective employment of those methods. The notion that "orientation" might be fundamental rather than incidental appears to have attracted little support.

During the succeeding decade, the emphasis given to insurgency and the specifics of dealing with low-intensity conflict fluctuated somewhat from year to year, but the importance given to them never approached the level given to more highly orchestrated warfare of a conventional or nuclear sort. That low-intensity conflict was actually high-stakes warfare gained support among specialists, but it was a difficult argument to make throughout the armed forces or even throughout the Army. The Security Assistance course offered by the CGSC Department of Strategy did attempt to provide a history of insurgencies and their organization, and to compare current and potential cases where nation-building and insurgency could be seen in competition. But the concerns advanced in this course do not appear to have been reflected in courses on staff operations, leadership and management, tactics, and logistics (offered by the departments of Command, Tactics, and Logistics). To this extent, the efforts by the Department of Strategy may have appeared somewhat as ideas lacking the firm anchor of institutionalized material support. Similarly, although there was some effort to bring to Fort Leavenworth speakers who could suggest alternate "strategies for the 1970s" (Roger Hilsman and George Ball, for example), residual antipathy toward speakers seen as compromised by their relationship to events in Vietnam probably undermined the authority of their presentations.[7]

In the 1974–75 and 1975–76 academic years at CGSC, Vietnam explicitly made its way into the curriculum, albeit in a comparatively modest fashion. Vietnam was the object of a two-hour case study within the comprehensive course in strategic studies in the first of those years; and in the second, the Vietnam experience was included within a course on "Tactical Lessons of 20th Century Wars."[8] Still, compared to the overwhelming bulk of studies officially sanctioned in the CGSC curriculum, insurgency and low-intensity conflict appeared to be the secondary players. Vietnam itself also appears to have been a difficult topic to place suitably within formal studies.

Course content at CGSC in 1976–77 included both new and old components, yet the trend did not favor a focus on the issues embedded in the Vietnam experience. Security Assistance and Unconventional Warfare were retained within the general course, Studies in Low-Intensity Conflict. Unconventional Warfare also continued as a specialized elective while Procedures for Conduct of Air-Land Battle (Course 1602) reached the status of a full course. In all, this largely evolutionary process within the official curriculum continued in 1977–78; and synthesizing innovations such as

AirLand Battle (a novelty despite having roots in pre-1960s Army concerns) were pressed forward even while the terminology of *low-intensity conflict* made its way into official descriptions of the CGSC program. From one perspective, the evolution suggested that interest in conventional warfare concerns overbalanced the interest in low-intensity conflict, even without having fully attended to the latter as experienced in Vietnam.[9] By 1978–79, low-intensity conflict had lost some of its separate identity and was subsumed under the Joint, Combined, and Special Operations course. A limited opportunity to search the recent past for relevant historical lessons survived in Evolution of Twentieth Century Tactics, which was embedded within the Applied Military History course. Courses that suggested irregular forms of conflict—the course on terrorism introduced in 1978–79, for example—actually reflected concerns over the NATO region, the Middle East, and other areas where conventional capabilities could be threatened by terrorist action. Concern over terrorism was tied appreciably, if not exclusively, to a concern over conventional forces.[10]

The CGSC curriculum during the 1970s did not suggest a strong official commitment to analyzing Vietnam. In fact, the official emphasis on matters other than Vietnam, low-intensity conflict, and insurgency created the very real possibility that a gap would develop between course content and student interests. One example: in spring 1975, the official CGSC program included a seminar on officer responsibility. Special guest participants included representatives from the press and electronic media, from universities, from the clergy, and from various constituent groups. As the seminar progressed, the Army officer-students drew an increasingly specific focus on Vietnam and its enigmas. This tendency, evidently driven by the personal experiences of the officers, was immensely strengthened by the military and political collapse of South Vietnam, which occurred during the same days as the seminar. Discussion in formal settings, as well as outside them, attended to little other than Vietnam; and fragmentary information suggests that this general discrepancy between official interest and student interest appeared in varying degrees throughout the 1970s.

In the early 1980s, as the Army began to develop a view of the Vietnam experience that made it seem less enigmatic, CGSC gave somewhat greater formal recognition to Vietnam. And since professional military educational programs tend to be shaped by a perception of what is important, the increased visibility of Vietnam as an object of formal study evidenced its pertinence to the Army's present business rather than its merely having retracted far enough into the past to be a "safe" area. In the 1982–83 program, Case Studies in US Military Intervention since 1898 explicitly included consideration of Vietnam; History of Air Warfare was partly devoted to air power's relevance to Vietnam; and—more broadly—emphasis on events, forces, and personalities that influenced the Army received formal sanction.[11] CGSC saw the official organization of the Combat Studies

Institute (CSI) in July 1979, which gave somewhat greater definition to the effort to provide a historical framework that included unpleasant events that had been important to the development of the Army—even events that were challenging to doctrine.[12] This is not to say that the Army's embrace of history as a discipline or Vietnam as a lesson was unqualified; but it did suggest that, at least to some extent, the discrepancy between formally and actually important issues was lessened. A course on The American Experience in Vietnam appeared in the curriculum for 1983-84—hardly dominating the attentions of faculty and students, but at least taking a place among various important forces that had shaped the Army.[13] On the other hand, CSI's specialized studies did not include analyses dealing with Vietnam. If emphasis placed on specific kinds of forces and force structures was something of a pendulum, it still had not swung away from interest in heavier units. Vietnam's real importance lay in its detrimental effect on an educational enterprise still concentrating on heavy regular units and on the status of units stationed in high-value areas such as Europe.[14]

In retrospect, one may detect phases in CGSC's treatment of Vietnam. Even while the war in Vietnam was a pressing problem, it lacked official endorsement as a high-priority issue worthy of study on its own terms. Only gradually did Vietnam receive an official place in the curriculum—and then because the United States government began to give serious consideration to possible involvements in countries where low-intensity and irregular-force scenarios were likely. What remained uncertain during the early 1980s was whether any new involvements could be based firmly on local conditions.

Spreading the Word

The promulgation of official and quasi-official viewpoints within the schools was complemented by the work of military journals, usually resident at forts and bases where the schools were located. These publications provided a kind of extension program to a wider and more diverse community interested in defense matters. In publications such as the *Naval War College Review*, the Army War College's *Parameters*, and the *Air University Review*, military and civilian writers have sought to learn some lessons from the past, make sense out of the present, and get some grasp on the future. Disclaimers are standard fare, emphasizing that all opinions expressed are the opinions of the authors alone. These journals nevertheless provided an indication of what editorial boards, advisers, and journal staffs regarded as worthwhile issues. Approval of an essay for publication qualified as a kind of tentative endorsement of the worth of the argument, even if it did not necessarily mean agreement with it.

From the end of US combat participation in the Vietnam War through the threshold of the 1980s, the *Naval War College Review* published articles on a broad range of topics. Relatively few of them, however, related to counterinsurgency or low-intensity conflict; and few related explicitly to the recent Vietnam War. For example, only one of 37 full-length articles published in the *Naval War College Review* from mid-1972 through mid-1973 dealt with Vietnam—and then largely in the context of legal responsibility for actions taken by one's subordinates.[15] Three articles dealt in detail with issues pertaining to low-intensity conflict or to irregular warfare, but these did not always concentrate on Vietnam as a source of information.[16] The preponderance of articles ranged over such issues as the defense budget, management techniques and policy, civil-military relations in other countries, and international law and the law of the sea. Breadth and diversity were considerable, and the "long view" on important issues was clearly present. If a problem might be cited, perhaps it was difficulty in gaining a dispassionate long view on so close an experience as Vietnam.[17]

The subsequent year's offerings were directed largely toward strategic issues such as the oil crisis, assessment of Soviet military policy, professionalism in the military, the prospects of a multipolar world after the 1980s, and possible instability in the balance of power among the major states. Only one article explicitly dealt with Vietnam: Rear Adm James B. Stockdale's reflections on his experience as a prisoner of war.[18] Explicit reference to Vietnam in the journal's mid-1974 through mid-1975 issues came in an article on motivation among US prisoners of war held in North Vietnam during the war.[19] Figures of some note during the Vietnam War contributed essays, though not focused on that experience: Walt W. Rostow returned to themes of political economy and scarcity; and Philip Geyelin, editorial commentator for the *Washington Post*, discussed the role of the press in American society.[20]

A number of articles published in the *Naval War College Review* from mid-1975 through mid-1976 focused on defense issues related to détente and on broad issues of military professionalism. Examples are Helmut Sonnenfeldt's "The Meaning of 'Détente'" (Summer 1975) and Dale R. Herspring's "The Effect of Détente on Professionalism and Political Control in the East German Army" (Winter 1976). But the largest single group of articles studied specific cases and incidents, ranging from the US naval presence in the Middle East through citizen participation in the Swedish army to the relationship of the Cuban missile crisis of 1962 to the development of Soviet naval forces.[21] Only two of 31 full-length articles pertained to low-intensity conflict or to Southeast Asia.

In the *Naval War College Review*'s 29th volume, from mid-1976 through mid-1977, the Vietnam War made a limited appearance with an article-length commentary on Gareth Porter's *A Peace Denied* and an essay on national security models with reference to the Vietnam experience.[22] But four articles dealt explicitly with the emergence of the Soviet navy as a major force in world affairs and five articles dealt explicitly with Middle Eastern problems, including the strategic importance of oil supply and the resource's potential vulnerability.[23] Of over 165 articles from mid-1977 through mid-1980, only three dealt with Vietnam in a major way—and these on the suitability of the code of conduct and on prisoner of war issues. If anything, direct and frontal treatment of the Vietnam War and issues directly stemming from it had declined. Moreover, although regional problems and their security implications received generous attention, there appeared to be no increase of interest in specialized methods that might be received in those areas. The focus was still essentially on the "big picture"— the very big picture.

If any one theme did stand out, beyond the understandable interest in current and likely future responsibilities, it was the focus on naval issues. In this, the *Naval War College Review* was substantially like its counterparts produced by the other services. By the end of the 1970s, for example, the *Air University Review* was publishing occasional essays on aspects of the Vietnam War; and a few *Air University Review* authors made use of events in the Vietnam conflict to illustrate their arguments about other regions or about specific topical matters.[24]

Also, like its counterpart journals, the *Naval War College Review* saw something of a movement "back to the basics." Although this was exemplified by an occasional piece on such hallowed strategic theorists as Alfred Thayer Mahan and Carl von Clausewitz, it was much more frequently presented in articles on the basic issues those theorists raised.[25] Traditional perspectives on war and precepts for its conduct were staging a comeback. Although the works of Clausewitz do not support a unitary vision of war and can easily encompass great diversity in tactics and methods, the resort to Clausewitz's formulations suggested a reassertion of the worth of professional military experience and of the trustworthiness of professional military judgment. Such a restoration of self-confidence was more than welcome. The question was whether it would ask too much of other official constituencies—or of the public on whose support the military would ultimately have to depend.

Training and Learning

To the extent that common ground appeared among the services on the meaning of the recent past, it included an overwhelming interest in method and technique. The reassertion of professional expertise thus took a largely traditional tack, aiming to identify principles and placing great emphasis on the integrity of military operations. This approach also sharpened the seeming attention to standard procedure and paralleled the underlying preference to play one's strong suit.

Such notions showed themselves in the curricula of the various service schools and in the several publications sponsored by the armed forces. Nor were these notions confined to the military; numerous constituencies, both in and out of the defense community, made their separate peace with the events of the 1960s and 1970s. The underlying question was whether any genuine "learning" had occurred—certainly with respect to Southeast Asia and, perhaps, even more broadly.

In the schools of professional military education, the question was whether what was actually being accomplished was closer to reinforcement of doctrine or to training. In a lecture delivered at the Naval War College and published in the November–December 1973 issue of the *Naval War College Review*, Philip A. Crowl charted the relationship of education and training in the Navy's senior school between 1884 and 1972.[26] The issues Crowl identified had parallels in the higher schools of the other services as well. Among the most visible, and surely most enduring, was the intent of the whole enterprise. Apart from suspicions that the college was unduly elitist, its critics had tended to regard the school as excessively committed to broad philosophical concerns rather than practical ones. William S. Sims, for example, an aggressive and remarkedly gifted young officer who later served as president of the Naval War College, was less than eager to be assigned there as a student. He wrote to his wife in 1911: "It may even be that things will blow over to such an extent that I may get some duty I would like better—something in closer touch with practice and less on the theoretical side."[27]

Alfred Thayer Mahan, the most effective exploiter of historical experience in support of the US emergence as a naval power, was once asked by two other officers if the college's instructors were "going to do anything practical." When Mahan asked them to define the term, the answer was: "Well, torpedo boats and launches—and that sort of thing."[28] As Crowl points out, these sentiments mark the major controversy running through a century of professional military education.

> Reduced to its essence . . . it is broad-gauged, liberal education versus training in technical skills—it is strategic-level education versus basic professional training—it is the preparation of officers for the remote contingencies of naval and military leadership versus preparing them for the immediate responsibilities of their next tour of duty.[29]

The Naval War College, like the other senior service schools, shifted emphasis from time to time. Several factors account for the attractiveness of one emphasis over another in any given period. In the midtwentieth century, one of the most critical factors was the diversification and proliferation of recognized academic disciplines. Subfields of major disciplines broadened into full-fledged fields such as statistics and whole new fields such as computer science emerged. The expansion of knowledge was occurring at such a rate that it virtually became a qualitatively different force. By the middle of the nineteenth century, the expectation that prevailing wisdom would be supplanted by new knowledge within a short time increased sharply. Even in the influential realm of theoretical physics, new models for explaining the cosmos appeared with unsettling frequency.[30] One of the casualties, in the end, was much of the old certitude in military verities.

The proliferation of branches of knowledge and their acceptance as legitimate fields in their own right created a dilemma in military education no less than in civilian education: the task of determining what constituted the core of learning appropriate for the well-educated officer was obscured, just as the proliferation of disciplines in civilian institutions ate away the very concept of a *liberal education*.[31] The Naval War College elevated specialized areas into autonomous fields. Among the college's 13 special military chairs founded in 1969, for example, were those devoted to *airstrike warfare*, *surface strike warfare*, and *amphibious operations*. The final concern, allowing for the praise one might give to the desire to be thorough, was that the program suffered from "the superficiality of its coverage of most of the material pertaining to international relations, economics, sociology, et cetera. . . ."[32]

The return of interest in such military theorists as Mahan, Clausewitz, and Thucydides marked an effort to redress an imbalance on the technical side. In his December 1972 convocation address, Naval War College President Stansfield Turner rejected an excessive focus on "the brief period of military strategy since the close of World War II," suggesting that too narrow a view and too thin a cut would leave the military rootless.[33] In the end, then, the test of real accomplishment in learning was not the acquisition of a whole range of skills whose relevance would swiftly be overtaken by still newer technological advancements. It was, instead, the transformation of understanding and the enhancement of sensitivity in the officers who passed through the college. It was, to be sure, the highest test; in civilian institutions, only a minority of students passed it.

The return to historical perspective was something of a mark of progress, at least for some observers; but the real challenge was to give some concrete meaning to this process of appreciating the present through the vantages offered by the past. Just as recent experiences in which one has been deeply involved may seem extraordinarily rich and complex with possible meanings, so can historical experiences long removed from the present retain a tremendous openness to new understanding and reinterpretation. If one discovers nuances of understanding about the past in recent experience, how was such a past to serve as a stable basis for action in the present? How was the ordinary human being to deal with a past and a present that seemed to be reciprocally connected? Where was the firm ground? Establishing a concrete meaning for the past—and for military tradition—provided some hint of what a return to "the basics" might actually mean for the armed services and for defense more broadly.

The goals of the Naval War College, for example, as it undertook revision of the curriculum in strategy, emphasized the importance of affecting each student in a profound way. The curriculum had been revised "to enhance the student's ability to think analytically and express himself cogently by allowing him to examine key issues of military history in the give and take of the seminar room."[34] The use of historical perspective was intended "not so much as a means to derive certain 'principles,' but rather as a means to view controversial issues more objectively and dispassionately."[35] Such high goals, however, depended not only on the goodwill of the faculty and students but also—perhaps to a perilous degree—on the level of prior preparation and on a host of inclinations and predispositions brought into the study. The methodology for achieving the high goals of the new curriculum in strategy included a sharp turn away from lectures (167 hours under the previous curriculum versus 75 under the new one), a 250-percent increase in required reading, a sextupling of the total writing requirement, and the introduction of written examinations aimed at synthesizing the product of reading and discussion.[36] Still, the challenge remained a personal one—how would the individual student coming from a hectic assignment respond to all that "spare" time?[37] The question was what specific interpretative meaning drawn from the past would be attached to present problems.

In the end, it was not clear that the schools and the publications had had sufficient appropriate impact to ensure that a real breakthrough had taken place. The emphasis on techniques by which to cope with problems or through which to manage them may have left inadequate room for ways of resolving them. How to handle problems constituted a body of knowledge and skills surely worth knowing; but a deeper issue was to identify what the problems really were—to seek out the "problem beneath the problem," lest one be condemned to treating symptoms rather than their governing causes. To the extent that a deeper learning took place, it would likely have shown itself in a measured and somewhat detached assessment of current troubles that minimized the impulse to see them as unprecedented. But to the extent that techniques for putting out the flares of conflict before they widened into major war predominated, the threshold of a deeper education of one's self and one's service would not yet have been crossed; and school solutions could become part of a broader problem, even though the interpretation of the past which they embodied gave deceptive short-term aid and comfort to those whom it touched.

Notes

1. The entire course of 1,712 hours also included in-processing, out-processing, commandant's time, physical conditioning, and open time. Materials describing the CGSC curriculum include annual CGSC catalogs, programs of instruction (POIs), and after-action reports from course instructors. These are available through the Library, US Army Command and General Staff College, Fort Leavenworth, Kansas (hereafter cited as CGSC Library).

2. *US Army CGSC Catalog*, 1972–73, RB-1001-1, CGSC Library. Discussion of US policy toward Cambodia, including the 1970 "incursion" and the overthrow of Prince Norodom Sihanouk, centered on the decisionmaking process in Washington but not on fighting in the countryside involving such groups as the Khmer Rouge. The concept of wars of national liberation received some mention in a course on the Military Strategies of the People's Republic of China, POI R5330, CGSC Library.

3. POI R1306, Tactical Operations in the NBC Environment, CGSC Library, 19.

4. POI R3000, Tactics, CGSC Library.

5. POI R2035, Leadership—The Environment, CGSC Library.

6. POI R7270, The Military Adviser, CGSC Library; for related information see, POI R7320, Security Assistance Program, CGSC Library.

7. Course offerings are described in the *US Army CGSC Catalog*, 1973–74.

8. *US Army CGSC Catalog*, 1974–75, 1975–76. Among the texts used for the course in "Tactical Lessons . . ." was *Seven Firefights in Vietnam*, released by the Army's Office of the Chief of Military History (subsequently Center of Military History); and special attention was given to John A. Cash's essay, "Fight at Ia Drang."

9. *US Army CGSC Catalog*, 1977–78.

10. Ibid., 1978–79; also see, P613, "Evolution of Twentieth Century Tactics."

11. *US Army CGSC Catalog*, 1982–83, especially courses A626 and A835.

12. Ibid., 1978–79; see also, *US Army CGSC Catalog*, 1978–79; P613, "Evolution of Twentieth Century Tactics," 1–10.

13. Ibid., 1983–84, especially course A628.

14. Informal conversations, Combat Studies Institute personnel, 7 December 1983.

15. Lt Col Franklin A. Hart, "Yamashita, Nuremberg and Vietnam," *Naval War College Review* 25 (September–October 1972).

16. Lt Col Harold D. Gallagher, "Combat Support in Wars of National Liberation," *Naval War College Review* 25 (September–October 1972); Lyman B. Kirkpatrick, Jr., "Paramilitary Case Study—The Bay of Pigs," *Naval War College Review* 25 (November–December 1972); Lt Col Earl F. Pierson, "The United States Role in Counterinsurgency," *Naval War College Review* 25 (January–February 1973).

17. Lest the line of discussion here seem completely unfair, it is worth noting that "distance" comes primarily from attitude, stance, and disposition rather than from the passage of time. Similarly, one can retain a highly biased view despite the passage of time.

18. Rear Adm James B. Stockdale, "Experiences As a POW in Vietnam," *Naval War College Review* 26 (January–February 1974).

19. Comdr Robert J. Naughton, "Motivational Factors of American Prisoners of War Held by the Democratic Republic of Vietnam," *Naval War College Review* 26 (January–February 1975).

20. Walt W. Rostow, "Political Economy in a Time of Scarcity: Or How to Get from Here to There," *Naval War College Review* 27 (September–October 1974); Philip Geyelin, "The Role of the Press in an Open Society," *Naval War College Review* 27 (March–April 1975).

21. Helmut Sonnenfeldt, "The Meaning of 'Détente,'" *Naval War College Review* 18 (Summer 1975); Dale R. Herspring, "The Effect of Détente on Professionalism and Political Control in the East Germany Area," *Naval War College Review* 28 (Winter 1976); Comdr Peter W. DeForth, "U.S. Naval Presence in the Persian Gulf: The Mideast Force since World War II,"

Naval War College Review 28 (Summer 1975); William J. Stover, "National Defense and Citizen Participation in Sweden: The Citizen Army in an Open Society," *Naval War College Review* 18 (Fall 1975); Lt Comdr Harlan K. Ullman, "The Cuban Missile Crisis and Soviet Naval Development: Myths and Realities," *Naval War College Review* 28 (Winter 1976).

22. Lt Col Jean Sauvageot, "A Peace Denied: The United States, Vietnam and the Paris Agreements," *Naval War College Review* 29 (Winter 1977); Lt Col Huntley E. Shelton, "National Security Models and Vietnam," *Naval War College Review* 29 (Spring 1977).

23. On the Soviet navy, see Lt Comdr William R. Hynes, "The Role of the *Kiev* in Soviet Naval Operations," *Naval War College Review* 29 (Fall 1976); David J. Kenney, "A Primer on S. G. Gorshkov's Sea Power and the State," *Naval War College Review* 29 (Spring 1977); Thomas R. Maddux, "United States-Soviet Naval Relations in the 1930's: The Soviet Union's Efforts to Purchase Naval Vessels," *Naval War College Review* 29 (Fall 1976); Uri Ra'anan, "The Soviet View of Navies in Peacetime," *Naval War College Review* 29 (Summer 1976). Concerning Middle Eastern affairs, see Robert O. Freedman, "Soviet Policy toward the Middle East since the October 1973 Arab-Israeli War," *Naval War College Review* 29 (Fall 1976); Maj Robert H. McKenzie-Smith, "Crisis Decisionmaking in Israel: The Case of the October 1973 Middle East War," *Naval War College Review* 29 (Summer 1976); James P. Piscatori, "Saudi Arabia and the Law of the Sea," *Naval War College Review* 29 (Spring 1977); David A. Rosenberg, "The U.S. Navy and the Problem of Oil in a Future War," *Naval War College Review* 29 (Summer 1976).

24. See, for example, Joe P. Dunn, "Reflections on Vietnam: The Lessons?" *Air University Review* 31, no. 1 (November–December 1979): 102-6; Capt Earl H. Tilford, Jr., "Search and Rescue in Southeast Asia, 1961-1965," *Air University Review* 31, no. 2 (January–February 1980): 60-74; Donald J. Alberts, "Tactical Air Power within NATO," *Air University Review* 31, no. 3 (March–April 1980): 59-70; Lt Col George M. Hall, Jr., "When Honor Conflicts with Duty," *Air University Review* 31, no. 6 (September–October 1980): 45-60.

25. See, for example, Edward A. Thibault, "War As a Collapse of Policy: A Critical Evaluation of Clausewitz," *Naval War College Review* 25 (May–June 1973); Norman H. Gibbs, "Clausewitz on the Moral Forces in War," *Naval War College Review* 27 (January–February 1975); Michael T. Corgan, "Mahan and Theodore Roosevelt: The Assessment of Influence," *Naval War College Review* 33 (November–December 1980).

26. Philip A. Crowl, "Education versus Training at the Naval War College: 1884-1972," *Naval War College Review* 26 (November–December 1973): 2-10.

27. Ibid., 3. Also see, Elting E. Morrison, *Men, Machines, and Modern Times* (Cambridge, Mass.: MIT Press, 1966).

28. Ibid., 3.

29. Ibid., 4.

30. The notion of paradigms is developed at length in Thomas S. Kuhn, *The Structure of Scientific Revolutions* (Chicago: University of Chicago Press, 1970). On the technical inclination as it responded to Prussian military ideas, see Crowl, 5.

31. This is especially pertinent since military learning, for all the professions of its stakes as a science, still started from premises of understanding that were an essentially liberal art.

32. Crowl, 8. Also see John W. Moseland and Lawrence T. Roadway, *Soldiers and Scholars: Military Education and National Policy* (Princeton, N.J.: Princeton University Press, 1957); Edward H. Katzenbach, "The Demotion of Professionalism at the War Colleges," *Proceedings*, March 1965, 34-41.

33. Quoted in Crowl, 9.

34. "A Perspective of the College's Strategy Curriculum," *Naval War College Review* 25 (March–April 1983): 19.

35. Ibid., 20.

36. Ibid., 19.

37. A remark heard more than once concerning the Air War College curriculum was that

it was "three months' work crammed into a year." The Air War College program was aimed at encouraging discussion and group interaction, as was the Naval War College program, but the format and specific allocation of time differed significantly from those of the Naval War College.

CHAPTER 4

POST-VIETNAM EVENTS AND PUBLIC DISCOURSE

In 1967 revolutionary Che Guevara predicted that the United States would face "two, three . . . many Vietnams."[1] Yet, even as the conflict itself was composed of many kinds of war at different times and in different places, so has retrospective public discourse about Vietnam lacked coherence in almost every respect. The exception is a clear consensus that "something" went wrong in Vietnam and in American handling of Southeast Asian problems. But no comparable consensus emerged to identify that "something." Public discourse concerning the Vietnam War has thus taken for granted that the United States must avoid repeating what went wrong. But the judgment of what must be avoided has remained idiosyncratic and eclectic.

The Vietnam War is not unique in being reduced to a simple sentiment or attitude. In fact, this seems the destiny of all American wars. The process of failing to agree on most details of wars and rapidly forgetting the few that had been agreed on may have become especially strong during the past half century. Feelings have assumed more importance than thought, and what one ought to know about a war that is past matters less in the public mind than how one actually feels about it. The process of reaching conclusions logically by sorting through evidence has become tedious in an age when personality means more than political content. And so the extremely simplified understanding of a war in terms of plain sentiment—and usually only one sentiment at that—has become all but irrepressible.[2]

Typical of this process of simplification was the feeling that World War II was the "good" war.[3] Despite the extraordinary diversity and complexity of World War II, it was finally reduced to this single sentiment—not because individuals comprehended all the details of the wartime experience but rather because the war provided an emotionally understandable reference point for each person's own individual memories. So, too, if World War II was the "good" war, Vietnam became the "troubled" war, the "longest" war, and the "confused" war—if not exactly the "bad" war.[4] As with World War II, the individual could make a personal accommodation with the Vietnam War without needing a public agreement as to what had happened and what it meant.

How Vietnam was reconsidered during the decade after the war, then, depended largely on the sentiments of the individuals and the imperatives of each medium through which reappraisal was undertaken. In general, however, the mass communications media—both print and electronic—displayed a limited attention span when they finally undertook reexamination; and they rarely achieved any depth of coverage and insight. Apart from any question of editorial intent, the contours and limits of the mass media's historic memory of Vietnam derived from their own focus on the present. Yesterday's events quickly lost their legitimacy as news, and so their eligibility for coverage ended.[5]

Even if one chose to draw attention to Vietnam and to discover its lessons just a few years after the war's end, it would already have been necessary to spend precious time and space on a simple narration of events. Many viewers and readers would have forgotten much of what had happened; and many more would never have known. And for the critically important younger generation born during the Kennedy administration, the Vietnam experience was likely to be "ancient history" as much as the Peloponnesian War. It was bad enough that a common body of knowledge about the Vietnam War had not stabilized because of disagreement among its advocates and opponents. But matters became even worse when the absence of a common understanding also derived from an absence of common experience and shared memory. Thus, even ten years after US withdrawal from Vietnam, the American experience in Southeast Asia had become essentially the province of history rather than news; and the genuine retrieval of that experience required the slow disciplines of historical research and verification. Outside the specialized disciplines, however, recollection of Vietnam risked becoming a recital of the commentator's own dispositions and biases—true to the details of the war but false to its comprehensive appreciation years later. And like understanding of the Vietnam War itself, discussion of its pertinence to post-Vietnam events also became idiosyncratic and eclectic.

National Security Issues and the Post-Vietnam Press

As the usual round of national security issues developed during the years after US withdrawal from Vietnam, individual members of the press occasionally found cause to recall the lost venture. But consistent patterns of recollection and reference did not emerge. The Vietnam experience remained multifaceted and ambivalent; and even political inclination and ideology were faulty predictors of how Vietnam analogies would be used.

A common theme, especially by the 1980s, was the need to take action in foreign affairs, albeit in a reasoned manner. Some major newspapers suggested that the main lesson of the Vietnam experience was that the

United States must resist a "species of isolationism marked by a paralysis of will in the conduct of American foreign policy." Such was the view of the *San Diego Union* in an editorial titled "Another Vietnam?" published on 2 August 1983.[6] The *Union* disputed alleged similarities between Vietnam and current issues such as El Salvador and Nicaragua in either political or military matters. The only constant, according to the *Union*, was misapprehension of the administration's policies by their opponents. The *Union* alleged that critics of the administration had adopted an oversimplified blanket view that discounted details and provided no basis for taking concrete steps to reach larger goals.[7] Ironically, some opponents of the administration's policy saw a similar dynamic of misapprehension and oversimplification, although they believed it was the government's supporters who were guilty of it. It was not hard to believe that Vietnam had been a source of confusion and misapprehension and that it remained so. But while this view could not in itself prevent a repetition of the error, it left post-Vietnam policy and opinion makers substantially free to develop their own ideas and constituencies to support them. Whether they did so was up to them.

Not infrequently, columnists used Vietnam as evidence that Americans needed to make tougher, more realistic appraisals of their allies and adversaries than they had during the 1950s and 1960s. In August 1984, for example, syndicated columnist Jack Anderson referred to Vietnam in order to expose the "schoolboy crushes" that he thought Roman Catholic priests had on left-wing revolutionaries.[8] In the article "Naive Clerics Might Learn from Vietnam," Anderson argued that a more skeptical attitude toward the Vietnamese government might have helped pave the way for genuine reform and protection of Roman Catholic interests in South Vietnam. Suggesting a broad parallel, he urged that the priests now question the high-sounding claims of the left-oriented factions in Central America.[9] The real lesson of Vietnam, at least in this respect, was not to avoid involvement but to overcome naïveté. Political issues remained real, but dealing with them required more than political action. It called for a change in attitude and adjustment in personality traits. Nor was the objective to be prejudgmental of major political stances, such as favoring either intervention in or abstention from the affairs of other states. Later in 1983, for example, when Anderson discussed the reemergence of the Central American Defense Council (Condeca), he saw it as a means to let Washington "sit back, supply its allies and have no fear of a Central American 'Vietnam' in an election year."[10] But here, too, the prospect of a Vietnam-like failure did not automatically mean either commitment or avoidance. It meant self-consciousness and caution.

Calls for tempering public discussion of foreign policy issues abounded. Marvin Stone editorialized in *U.S. News & World Report* on 21 March 1984 in favor of a middle ground on Central American issues, avoiding the "conflicting claims . . . , hyperbole and rhetoric" coming from both principal sides debating the problem. Stone denigrated the Vietnam analogy and the notion that it should prove persuasive in current affairs. Few Americans would gladly accept Soviet influence in Central America, Stone argued, but "fewer believe they face a choice between another Vietnam on the one hand and a catastrophic surrender of vital U.S. interests on the other."[11] The prospect of intervening did not trouble Stone, but making a specific commitment to do so under the influence of misleading debate did. He railed against exaggeration that gave "little help in understanding the realities of the US predicament in Central America."[12] Stone had no doubt of a government's right to intervene in extreme situations, but he demanded that reason and balance prevail in discussing when to do so.

Some who criticized US policies accepted the principle of active overseas commitments but challenged the logic of certain specific undertakings. Vietnam could be mentioned—but not as a blanket denial of the need for US action overseas. In "Echoes of Vietnam," published in the *Baltimore Sun* on 30 September 1983, Garry Wills allowed some similarity between the current US approach in Lebanon and the prior US action in Vietnam; but he specifically disavowed a "knee-jerk" comparison. His criticism focused on the reluctance of governmental figures to think concretely and to speak openly on public issues. He charged "official lies and evasions," and he dismissed congressional authorization of an 18-month US troop presence in Lebanon as a "shameful 'compromise' by which Congress tried to escape its duty to prevent undeclared wars."[13] Wills rejected rationales that were so sweeping that they could not be tested. In Lebanon, he reasoned, the United States could not leave "because that would be leaving," just as in Vietnam "our reason for being there was being there."[14] He assumed that military intervention could be justified in certain circumstances, but he could never justify it by mere "circular reasoning."[15] Again, the "legacy of Vietnam" was not "knee-jerk" avoidance but an impulse to critically examine the nation's commitments and involvements.

Although some officials claimed that their opponents were "ganging up" and raising the ghost of Vietnam, some highly visible critics conspicuously avoided it. Indeed, George W. Ball—one of the most strenuous opponents of US policy in Vietnam—wrote and spoke of American interests and actions in Lebanon and the Middle East without mentioning Southeast Asia at all. In "Why Is the US in Lebanon?" published in the *Christian Science Monitor* on 23 December 1983, Ball concentrated on the need to think concretely about Lebanese matters and to avoid acting on the basis of mere abstractions and generalities.[16]

Later events—notably the terrorist bombing of US Marine barracks at Beirut International Airport—heightened public questioning of the steps being taken by the US government in the Middle East. Public statements issued by the Reagan administration promised appropriate response to the guilty parties. But who was guilty? Writing in the *Washington Post* in October 1983, Philip Geyelin thought that US officials were failing to identify the specific parties responsible and so had no basis on which to pursue a selective policy. Geyelin's observation that Congress meanwhile sought a "less dangerous peace-keeping mission for the Marines" did not suggest tension between the goals of Congress and those of the president as much as Geyelin's emphasis on knowing concrete details about areas in which the United States was involved. Doing something well meant not doing things indiscriminately.

The lessons of Vietnam, for the editors of the *Baltimore Sun*, did not lie in some list of specific actions or specific policies but in a change of attitude. In an editorial titled "Vietnam, Lebanon, El Salvador," published on 24 February 1984, the *Sun* pointed toward "a cultural arrogance on both sides of the congressional debate" over Central America. The *Sun* cast doubt on "the administration's notion that 55 U.S. military advisers can transform the Salvadoran army into a law-abiding outfit dedicated to Western democratic principles...." But it also questioned whether "the United States can impose on Salvadoran society its own legalistic definitions of human rights." The editors asserted that the United States can retain its objectives in human rights and other areas; but it cannot expect to achieve them and should not act under the illusion that it can. "If this country has learned anything from Vietnam and Lebanon," they continued, "it should be an appreciation of a large outside power's incapacity to alter the essential nature of a smaller one." When the *Sun* allowed the existence of "ghosts" from Vietnam and Lebanon, it was in the intertwining of "ill-fated U.S. military entanglements and debatable strategic assessments."[17]

In various respects, the views presented by the *Sun* could be disputed. Depending on the respective size and power of the large and small countries, it might actually be possible to "alter the essential nature" of the smaller country, provided the time and practical means were available. Surely, the life or "nature" of the Republic of Korea was fundamentally changed in the decades after 1950 from that prevailing before World War II. Similarly, the experience of the southern part of Vietnam after US withdrawal suggests that substantial change may have been possible there too. And the changes in political direction on the small island nation of Grenada also moot the *Sun*'s claims.

But despite the criticisms one might lodge against the *Sun*'s editorial writers, there was an important element of neutrality in the view they espoused. There was no imperative either for or against intervention as a matter of principle. To the extent that there was any predetermined imperative, it was toward a cautionary respect for the hard facts of the real world outside America.

In denying that Vietnam had pertinence to the continuing national security interests of the United States, writers meant "pertinence" in a narrow sense—that no specific measures could be transplanted from one region to another; and a broader one—that old attitudes ought not to hobble Americans in new situations. Writing in the *Washington Times* on 24 January 1984, for example, Philip Gold speculated that Vietnam provided few lessons. He wrote that "as a guide to future individual and national conduct, it offers no guidance at all."[18] Still, Gold enumerated ways of doing business in Vietnam that he believed caused American failure there: determining foreign policy on the basis of domestic political concerns, micromanagement of the war (often by persons professionally unqualified to attempt it), reduction of popular political discourse to "individual emotional states," and a "mindlessness" in conducting the war as well as in evaluating it.[19] Thus, while denying that Vietnam provided guidance, Gold enumerated its lessons. And however much he thought himself at odds with the general assessment of Vietnam being made by others, Gold shared their interest in how Americans behaved—in matters of character, disposition, inclination, and personality—even more than in how constraints created outside the United States affected US action in Southeast Asia. The greatest source of future guidance for US policy and its implementation, then, was less the record of events in Asia than the reflection on personality in America.

Leaders and Their Memories

From among Vietnam's effects on post-Vietnam events, one might usefully separate those consequences that are carried within the memories and personalities of leaders from those being forced on them against their will. In some cases, this must be a "close call." External pressures can exist. But deciding when it is the internal impulse and the internalized perception that is really at work remains difficult. It may be that charging others with excessive slavishness to the memories of Vietnam actually suggests something about oneself as much as about others. In any event, the decade after US withdrawal from Vietnam saw some readjustment in how US governmental and military leaders approached national security issues as well as an adjustment in opinions about the leaders themselves.

Although US withdrawal from Vietnam and Cambodia suggested a decline in American self-confidence, President Gerald Ford moved swiftly to prevent an obsessive "Vietnam syndrome" from paralyzing the nation. Ford justified his decision to use force to free the crew of the commercial vessel *Mayaguez* from Cambodian authorities because it might give a "shot in the arm" to the public, boosting their enthusiasm and confidence after the battering they had taken, especially in Vietnam.[20] Problems would persist, and debate over the lessons of Vietnam would continue. But Ford sought to make clear that total abstention from using military force was impossible.

News reporters occasionally revealed a kind of sympathy for public officials who felt improperly restrained by the lingering thoughts of the lost war in Vietnam. Secretary of Defense Caspar Weinberger proved an interesting example. Periodic reports appeared that "Weinberger and the military are afflicted with the 'Vietnam syndrome': a reluctance to flex American military muscles without substantial, advance political backing at home." So claimed Leslie H. Gelb in an extended article in the *New York Times* on 7 November 1983. Gelb, himself a former government official, said the Pentagon was frustrated by the State Department for "providing little policy guidance for the use of force and that vague goals like 'peace and stability' in Lebanon are a recipe only for open-ended involvement."[21]

Although one could explain the reticence of Weinberger and the top brass in terms of technical military requirements, outside observers did not always see it that way. Then, too, some of Weinberger's own published remarks lent fuel to the engines of suspicion. In an interview with Suzanne Garment, capital reporter for the *Wall Street Journal*, Weinberger troubled over what he believed was a change in the mood of Americans since the 1960s. "Vietnam and Watergate," he was quoted in the 5 August 1983 of the *Journal*, "did very serious damage to the United States and its potential foreign policy, and it will probably be a considerable period of time before we can recover from that experience...."[22] In some respects, Weinberger's position invited quarrel. The Vietnam experience gave an especially worrisome setting for the Reagan administration's programs more than it caused skepticism toward those policies. Also refutable was the secretary's implication that a bipartisan pursuit of American foreign policy was normal outside the framework of the cold war and its highly unusual impulse toward consensus. But the secretary clearly represented not only administration thinking on Vietnam but—more than he may have realized—thinking outside the administration as well in wanting to act "in ways that aren't heavily influenced by what occurred there."[23] The aim was to act without substantial reference to Vietnam; and, although there was disagreement on what positive new steps must be taken, putting Vietnam off into the past was an accepted element of a "new normalcy."

At times, eminent officials, whether past or current, accepted US involvement in potentially perilous international affairs by protesting a supposed fixation on Vietnam by their political opponents. Former Chief of Naval Operations Elmo Zumwalt and Worth Bagley accused Democrats of inventing a "One Answer" game in which all "complex foreign policy issues [receive] only one ambiguous clue in response: Vietnam." In "Vietnam and the Games Pols Play," published in the *Washington Times* on 12 August 1983, Zumwalt and Bagley sought to tie use of the Vietnam analogy to the

Democrats, referring to "loud, vacuous Democratic voices."[24] Still, even here, Zumwalt and Bagley's main thrust was to enumerate geopolitical considerations that made Central America a legitimate area of interest for the United States and one in which military operations were more practicable.[25]

Two writers for the *Washington Post* argued that administration officials were among those actually responsible for suggesting similarities between current US interests, such as those in El Salvador, and Vietnam; and they asserted that such suggestions came from every political quarter. In an article in the 11 March 1983 issue of the *Post* titled "El Salvador Isn't Vietnam," Stephen S. Rosenfeld noted that administration officials were prone to use metaphors and vocabulary from the Vietnam experience. He suggested that US officials speaking about El Salvador were "pushing buttons meant to elicit a certain mechanical response," even though "no usable consensus yet exists [concerning Vietnam] from which Americans might draw a common meaning" to apply to other problem areas. Rosenfeld believed that President Reagan himself "recognized the evocative power of 'Vietnam' by summoning up all the geopolitical specters he associates with the world in order to build support for his policy, even while denying ('there is no parallel whatsoever with Vietnam') the prospect of a widening war."[26] So, too, in a companion article titled ". . . But There Is a Chilling Resemblance," Philip Geyelin saw a connection, "not between the exact nature or likely dimension of El Salvador and Vietnam, but between the mindset, the strategic concept and the language of the policymakers then and now."[27] Neither writer saw intervention or the use of the military as a sufficient issue in itself; rather the debate must center on when such actions were justifiable as tested against real US interests, whether in Central America or Southeast Asia.

Senator John Stennis, an advocate of a relatively large military and a strong defender of the War Powers Act, took a similar view. The general pattern of US interests must be understood, and some broad sense of how to pursue those interests needed to be shared widely. He implied that a consensus must prevail if a war is to be undertaken successfully, arguing that one thing Vietnam had shown was the need for congressional approval to wage war. In an article published in *USA Today* on 19 September 1983, Stennis recalled his anxiety over waging war in Korea without a declaration; and he remembered that he had sought a declaration as the United States became deeply involved in Southeast Asia. "During the Vietnam War," he added, "I worked with experienced and wise members of the Senate who would ask the question over and over: 'How did we get into this war?'"[28] And so he insisted that after the war a satisfactory provision be made to retain the congressional power to determine that a commitment to war had been made. A key lesson of Vietnam, then, at least for Stennis, was that a war needed some genuine authorization, some clear starting point. Phrased the other way around, the United States should never have to guess how it got into a situation—it should be able to know. This concern for the mechanism of commitment, however, in no way predetermined whether the United States should commit to an intervention or abstain from it.

The *Chicago Tribune* also expressed concern that overt or implicit reference to Vietnam would distort debate over current problems. In an editorial on 18 March 1983, for example, the *Tribune*'s editorial writers stated boldly that "El Salvador Is Not Vietnam." The paper rejected what it saw as the administration's effort to "resurrect" the domino theory, while it belittled comparisons made by the administration's critics between the presence of US military advisers in El Salvador and their earlier presence in Vietnam. "The United States has a legitimate role to play in the struggles now going on in Central America," the editorial affirmed. "The Vietnam slogans are only cluttering up people's thinking about it."[29] Again, the view which emerged was that, although the government had no right to expect unthinking support of a crusade, it did have the right to pursue a reasoned defense of concrete interests by realistic means.

Various candidates aspiring to national office were at pains to show that they were not prisoners of Vietnam and to profess willingness to use force overseas when necessary. In the campaign for the Democratic presidential nomination in 1984, for example, Walter Mondale claimed better credentials for the Oval Office by suggesting that he was more willing than Gary Hart to use military force. Mondale clearly viewed this inclination as a positive one that appealed to the public. He specifically asserted that "guilt is not a foreign policy," implying that a generalized ethical test was a poor test of foreign policy.[30] Ethics and ideals were by no means irrelevant. In fact, they were necessary—but they were not sufficient. In pertinent concrete expression, values could be useful; but holding sway as abstractions, they were lethal snares.

Mondale claimed to oppose the "basic premise, direction and policies of the Reagan administration in Central America," and he insisted on progress in human rights as a precondition for continuing support to El Salvador. But opposition evidently had distinct limits. Mondale allowed that he might maintain US military personnel in Honduras. Moreover, he made clear that "power politics" would be the name of the game if he were elected, saying that the troops in Honduras would be a bargaining chip to press for Cuban withdrawal from Nicaragua. And although Senator Hart claimed to have long since opposed the stationing of US Marines in Beirut, Hart had actually sponsored a bill allowing a six-month extension of their presence there at a time when the Republicans in the Senate were pressing for an 18-month authorization. The same Democratic alternative, in fact, had also been backed by Mondale.[31]

It is interesting to note also that Senator Hart, in his role as a member of the Military Reform Caucus in Congress, implied that the United States had not exactly lost in Vietnam, even though it had clearly not quite won. In an article on the reformers published in the *New York Times*, Charles Mohr quoted Hart as saying reform would come slowly because change is not undertaken "without suffering a military defeat. The reform movement is seeking the change without the defeat."[32] This was hardly a case of wallowing in the depths of the Vietnam experience.

Even when referring to Vietnam as a source of guidance for current affairs, however, Gary Hart was inspired partly by Ronald Reagan, responding to the president's reference to Vietnam as "our finest hour." In a campaign ad published in March 1984, Hart urged that "the commitment of U.S. military force to Central America cannot be the answer to the problems in Central America, as it was not the answer in Vietnam."[33] Even here, however, Hart acknowledged that the use of force was a reasonable option when it was not "inappropriate." The key was to find the appropriate solutions to concrete problems. In the end, even for Hart—who distanced himself further from US governmental policy than Mondale did—opposition to the Reagan administration's conduct of foreign affairs was not a "knee-jerk reaction" caused by obsession with Vietnam. In a joint interview in New York on 1 April 1984, Hart spoke more broadly of "the error of Vietnam and Lebanon." The alleged problem was not Vietnam in specific but the more generic one of using force without clarity of purpose and predictability of result.[34] Pushed far enough, no political figure could avoid admitting force as a viable option. The issues were sufficiency of cause, frequency of use, intensity of force, and duration of commitment.

Vietnam in Public Memory

A decade after the collapse of the regime in South Vietnam, the American war in Southeast Asia had begun to assume a place in public memory that resembled, in significant respects, the place that previous American wars occupied. Although the Vietnam War may be the first major US defeat, it was hardly the first controversial war. The War of 1812 had brought the young nation to the edge of ruin, as New England states threatened secession. The American Civil War grew out of differences so deep that an end to military conflict could not possibly have settled them. It was possible to "agree to disagree" on many matters such as the causes of conflict, the justice of one's cause, or the nobility of one's motives. At long last, rallying around old virtues of dedication, loyalty, and sacrifice could transcend all specific political and military questions. Sentiments and sentimentality did not need the support of logical syllogisms. Narrow cerebral logic mattered less than the demands and instincts of the heart.

Perhaps the key symbol of those emotive instincts was the Vietnam Veterans Memorial, pioneered and built by a voluntary organization on prize federal property adjacent to the Lincoln Memorial. Initial reaction to the project ranged widely. Some were enthusiastic to remember the sacrifices of those who served, others were angry at memorializing what they considered a politically wrong-headed war. The design that won the competition stressed simplicity, consisting of two black granite walls receding below ground-level in a wide V-shape. The uproar was intense, as some denounced it as an "open grave" and an insult to those who had served. Others alleged that the V-shape imitated the V-sign that had been a symbol of the antiwar movement of the Vietnam era. Yet the designer's intention was only to set each wall on axis with a great patriotic monument—one with the Washington Monument, the key symbol of national unity and purpose, and the other with the Lincoln Memorial, the single greatest national symbol of sacrifice in the pursuit of freedom.

In time, a consensus of acceptance grew around the Vietnam Veterans Memorial. Its dedication became a symbol of national reconciliation. And rightly so. For this was the first national monument to engrave in memory the names of common soldiers, sailors, and airmen. The black granite walls were covered with the names of those who had fallen in the American campaigns in Vietnam, and each was recognized as a hero and patriot for the dedication and sacrifice given in the pursuit of duty. Political assessment of the Vietnam War itself was intentionally avoided. There was no need to decide even gross political questions such as whether the war had been a noble pursuit of freedom for one's friends or an imperialist adventure since the celebration of personal virtue pushed aside the search for political consensus.[35]

In New York City, public reconciliation with the Vietnam experience was symbolized by the building of a memorial honoring the war's veterans. The design selected was a 14-foot high glass wall, accented by two portals, with excerpts from letters, poems, and songs etched into the glass blocks. "We're not looking for fancy prose or edited letters," said a member of the winning design team. They sought real words expressing the deep emotions of the common soldier. New York City Mayor Edward Koch remarked: "What I like is its simplicity, and the fact that what will appear on the wall will be the comments of those who suffered." Significantly, Koch recognized the suffering and dedication of the American soldier, while so much of the attention during the war itself had been focused on harm done to noncombatants. "These comments," Koch added, "will be a constant reminder of how much we owe the dead and how much we owe the living."[36] Koch's words exemplified the movement of Vietnam from analysis into acceptance beyond assessment of the war's purpose to an appreciation of those who conducted it.

Empathy for those who participated in the war emerged in popular music, where appreciation of the veteran superseded acceptance of the war's politics. The highly successful singer and composer Bruce Springsteen set the balance in "Born in the U.S.A.," enumerating the concrete problems of the veteran, yet paradoxically knitting him back into the society. Less a cry of protest than one of pain, such songs strengthened the sentimental romance with "small town America" and the sense of home.[37]

Prime-time television programming generated the series "Magnum, P.I.," featuring a sometimes reflective Vietnam veteran and Naval Reserve officer as its principal character. The hero of the short-lived series "Call to Glory" was even an active duty Air Force officer; and the series was set in the era of the Vietnam War.[38] Meanwhile, the Public Broadcasting System (PBS) developed and presented an extensive series, "Vietnam: A Television History," presenting the varied points of view from almost all sides in the war. Even here and in the book published as a companion to the television series, human qualities—whether frailty or endurance, confusion or vision—served as the balm to ease and transcend the hurt of reviewing the experience.[39] In any event, one night's audience for the successful network series "Magnum" exceeded the accumulated audience of the entire run of the PBS series.

Films concerning the Vietnam War became ever more similar in tone to those spun off other American wars. Subtlety died as patriotic commitment resumed its traditional status as a high virtue. To be sure, early films—including some made during the war itself—sometimes preached specific political lessons, whether "prowar" or "antiwar." Notable for its bluntness, as well as its artistic failings, was *The Green Berets* (1968), which praised both the activities of US Special Forces and the basic US commitment to the Saigon government. On the other side of the political line, *Coming Home* (1978), extensively presented the views of the antiwar activists, even in explicit speeches delivered by Oscar-winner Jon Voight. Yet the underlying focus even in this film was concern for the Americans who had fought in Vietnam as much as for the Vietnamese. While clearly hostile to the political views that led the United States into war, *Coming Home* nonetheless hinted at the area in which a final accommodation among "prowar" and "antiwar" factions would emerge—an area beyond politics and dominated by personal concerns and human relationships.

Even as early as Michael Cimino's Academy Award-winning *The Deer Hunter* (1978), attention was shifting away from the political dimensions of the war and toward the human impact on those who served in Vietnam and on their families. Graced by convincing performances from first-rate actors, *The Deer Hunter* was nearly "unreadable" in political terms (its final scene even including a sincere rendition of the song "God Bless America"); but it drew from the audience a deep empathy with a broad range of characters who had suffered greatly and in varying ways. Similarly, Francis Ford Coppola's *Apocalypse Now* (1979), sometimes falsely called an "antiwar" film, actually used the Vietnam experience to see the sources of destructive behavior not within a political system but within human nature.

Drawn freely from Joseph Conrad's *The Heart of Darkness*, Coppola's *Apocalypse Now* delivered not a political statement but a personal one.

Quintessential "B-movies" of the 1980s carried the "prowar" faction's message that the US military forces had "had their hands tied" and "weren't allowed to win" in Vietnam. But the insistent, repeated theme of prisoners of war again revealed that the final resolution could not be made in political terms nearly as effectively as in human ones. While many Americans might still challenge the reasoning behind sending US military personnel to Southeast Asia, virtually none would dare challenge the sentiment to bring them all home. Thus, films such as *First Blood* (1982) introduced the more contentious analysis of the war itself, even as later films such as *Rambo* (1984) extended the concern for recovering Americans missing in Southeast Asia. But the inherent structural message of both such films was the primacy of the sentiments and instincts of the individual over the calculations of government. Political absolutes proved intractable. But one might always search out a workable, reasonable accommodation in human relationships, no matter how boldly it defies logic.

Thought and Feelings

The ultimate impact of Vietnam on post-Vietnam events may be largely a product of feelings, which hold a much stronger sway over public sentiment than does logical thought. And the news reporters and commentators—even the most diligent among them—may find it impossible to pull the public away from those deep feelings that are so much more compelling than syllogistic reasoning. Even political commentators and members of the press respected by the public may have only little impact if they deviate from the tide of public feeling.

The tendency to attribute to the Vietnam experience much more than was proved may well intensify. But it is not clear that this would finally alter the nature of long-term public discourse concerning Vietnam. Supposed lessons may be cited and recited until repetition creates an air of certitude. The "lessons of Vietnam" may emerge as boldly and as simplistically as the "lessons of Munich," smudging over the complexities and uncertainties of the experience. In general, however, the shape of the Vietnam memory has already substantially been formed—whether one calls it a need for clarity, a need for concreteness, or any of a host of other basically synonymous expressions. The memory is sustained less by fact and by detailed analysis than by long-standing impulses and inclinations among the people who carry it.

The enduring place of Vietnam in popular memory and public discourse depends less on Vietnam than on America—less on events in Southeast Asia than on attitudes and sentiments in the American people. In a way, this is only fair, since US policy in Vietnam was shaped substantially by forces welling up from America—projections from the American character. The concerns of the Vietnamese seemed less important to Americans than were the global interests of the United States, and the war in Vietnam was viewed in global terms at the expense of regional and local realities. This same attitude has proved dominant as Americans have come to establish a rhetoric of reference to Vietnam. It could hardly have been otherwise.

Notes

1. Article by Ernesto "Che" Guevara, Havana, Cuba, 16 April 1967, quoted in Daniel Smith, *Che Guevara* (New York: Stein and Day, 1969), 258.

2. Warren Susman has pointed out that Americans shifted emphasis from "character," which had concerned them in the nineteenth century, to "personality," which absorbed their attention in the twentieth century. This reflected a deeper turn away from public deliberation on political content in a logical fashion; and, in its place, personal feelings and one's "relationships" with others functioned as the new norm of behavior and as a new form of judgment. "Getting along" thus becomes more crucial than "getting things right," at least in any abstract sense. See Warren I. Susman, "'Personality' and the Making of Twentieth Century Culture," in Susman, *Culture as History* (New York: Pantheon Books, 1984).

3. Studs Terkel, *"The Good War": An Oral History of World War Two* (New York: Pantheon Books, 1984).

4. For example, see George Herring, *America's Longest War* (New York: Wiley and Sons, 1979).

5. This is not intended as a criticism of the mass media but only as a recognition of the imperatives created when one defines "news" in terms of currency of events rather than in terms of duration and depth of consequences.

6. "Another Vietnam?" *San Diego Union*, 2 August 1983.

7. Ibid.

8. Jack Anderson, "Naive Clerics Might Learn from Vietnam," *Washington Post*, 26 August 1983.

9. Ibid.

10. Jack Anderson, "Latin American Experts Fearful War Will Widen," *Washington Post*, 24 October 1983.

11. Marvin Stone, "El Salvador: Any Salvation?" *U.S. News & World Report*, 21 March 1983.

12. Ibid.

13. Garry Wills, "Echoes of Vietnam," *Baltimore Sun*, 30 September 1983.

14. Ibid.

15. Ibid.

16. George W. Ball, "Why Is the US in Lebanon?" *Christian Science Monitor*, 23 December 1983, 14.

17. "Vietnam, Lebanon, El Salvador," *Baltimore Sun*, 24 February 1984.

18. Philip Gold, "Vietnam: Doubts for the '80s," *Washington Times*, 24 January 1984.

19. Ibid.

20. Gerald R. Ford, *A Time to Heal* (New York: Harper and Row, 1979), 275-76.

21. Leslie H. Gelb, "Shultz, Pushing a Hard Line, Becomes Key Voice in Crises," *New York Times*, 7 November 1983, 1, 12.

22. Suzanne Garment, "Vietnam: It's Time for Cataloguing the Consequences," *Wall Street Journal*, 5 August 1983.

23. Ibid.

24. Elmo Zumwalt and Worth Bagley, "Vietnam and the Games Pols Play," *Washington Times*, 12 August 1983.

25. As suggested in a separate chapter of the present study, the restrictive association of Democrats with use of the Vietnam analogy is false. This does not imply insincerity on the part of Zumwalt and Bagley, but it may underscore the growing activism of the advocates of intervention.

26. Stephen S. Rosenfeld, "El Salvador Isn't Vietnam," *Washington Post*, 11 March 1983, 17. US Ambassador to the United Nations Jeane J. Kirkpatrick exemplified the administration's mix of using the Vietnam analogy while leaving it obscure when she asserted: "The biggest difference between Vietnam and Central America is the Pacific Ocean." Interview with Jeane Kirkpatrick, "This Week with David Brinkley," ABC television, 15 April 1984.

27. Philip Geyelin, ". . . But There Is a Chilling Resemblance," *Washington Post*, 11 March 1984, 17.

28. John Stennis, "Marines Could Be in a Spot Like Vietnam," *USA Today*, 29 September 1983.

29. "El Salvador Is Not Vietnam," *Chicago Tribune*, 18 March 1983.

30. Anthony Lewis, "Abroad at Home: The Democratic Quandary," *New York Times*, 22 March 1984.

31. Fay S. Joyce, "Mondale and Hart Clash on Central America," *New York Times*, 28 March 1984, 15.

32. Charles Mohr, "On Military: Debating Frills and Fundamentals," *New York Times*, 3 April 1984.

33. Gary Hart campaign advertisement, *New York Times*, 28 March 1984, 11.

34. "Excerpts From Candidates' New York Interviews," *New York Times*, 2 April 1984, 11.

35. The Vietnam Veterans Memorial has emerged as one of the most frequently visited of all sites in Washington, D.C.

36. David W. Dunlap, "A Wall to Honor Vietnam Veterans," *New York Times*, 30 May 1984, 12.

37. Bruce Springsteen, "Born in the U.S.A.," copyright 1984 Bruce Springsteen. Consistent with this "home-town" focus was the rhetoric of "coming home" popularized in the dedication of the Vietnam Veterans Memorial in Washington, D.C., and in related ceremonies.

38. The cancellation of the series "Call to Glory" owed much to its absence of a clear focus. Apparently, viewers had difficulty deciding if it was a "war story," a family story, or something else. Protest over the flattering portrayal of the Air Force pilot as hero did not develop.

39. The companion volume is Stanley Karnow, *Vietnam, A History* (New York: Viking Press, 1983).

CHAPTER 5

THE CONGRESS AND NATIONAL SECURITY AFTER VIETNAM: BUSINESS AS USUAL?

Issues pertinent to national security and the US military inevitably confront the US Congress. It must authorize and appropriate funds to support policy formulated by the executive branch. But Congress cannot escape making judgments on both the broad mechanisms for achieving national security objectives and the more specific options proposed for individual contingencies. The military's ability to work effectively with Congress, therefore, depends in some measure on the understanding each has of the other; and in the aftermath of the US experience in Vietnam, it is not certain that an understanding of the other party developed on either side. The roots of frustration thrive in the rich soil of misapprehensions, and a considerable measure of the frustration felt in various professional quarters appears to have been fanned by misunderstandings of the frequency, character, and thrust of references to the Vietnam War. At the same time, the legacy of assumptions and expectations left by Vietnam determines some of the rules of engagement between Congress and those who deal with it. It is clearly pertinent, then, to see what Vietnam's legacy appears to have been in the thinking of Congress and the legacy of thought that is imputed to Congress by outside parties. Finally, one should determine whether there is much correspondence between the two.

The Cold War Consensus and the Issue of "Normalcy"

How Congress was affected by Vietnam and how that change might affect the military's chances for achieving its goals in national security matters cannot be assessed without establishing a baseline of congressional thinking before Vietnam and a method for detecting difference. The baseline immediately preceding Vietnam was that of the cold war consensus under which a clearly bipartisan support for presidential guidance on foreign policy and national defense matters prevailed. Some have suggested that endorsement of the vision of the world as bipolar, in which anticommunism was seen as an inevitable component of a global confrontation, was the price paid by some for their own domestic liberalism. By maintaining an ardently anti-Communist stance, they could assure their political friends and foes that liberal social and economic policies were suitably American.[1] But the determination to rally in common cause overseas rose sharply in World War II against fascism; and it was not a disposition easily shaken, especially since the experience of World War II and disclosure of the full measure of Nazi atrocities confirmed the wisdom of antifascist unity.

On the other hand, a longer view of the American political tradition suggests that consensus on overseas matters has been far from the normative experience. Even during wars, division among Americans has been frequent and visible. When Americans were not in actual combat, linkages between foreign policies and domestic affairs were inescapable. Far from suppressing differences of view on external matters, Americans have often used matters of foreign relations as means of identifying alternate visions of what America itself ought to be.

Debate between the Federalists and Republicans, especially during the Adams and Jefferson administrations, on US relations with Great Britain and France and on the establishment of a deep-water naval capability represented differing inclinations as to the proper character of the American political system. This conflict is customarily seen as a difference in perception of central government authority. But it was also a divergence as to the wellsprings of American behavior. One side saw the United States role in world affairs as a response to challenges thrust upon the nation from outside while the other saw the actions of the United States as swelling from its chosen desires.[2]

A later and equally vigorous debate over annexation policies took place in and around the years of the US war with Mexico. Which lands to acquire from Mexico (or, for that matter, to secure by negotiating with Britain or Russia) was the reciprocal of a host of knotty domestic problems: whether the United States could tolerate multilingualism, whether it could overcome anticatholicism, and—most of all—how it could contain the increasing stresses of domestic slavery.[3] Late nineteenth-century expansionism similarly entailed a dispute over the American political character and over the sources of US conduct, again reinforcing the view that US actions overseas grew first from what Americans sought to achieve and only secondarily from the need to defend against other countries. For example, those who opposed annexation of Hawaii and US administration of the Philippines did not do so because of isolationism but because they feared that acquiring colonial possessions would fundamentally corrupt the US political system.[4] Debate and dissent concerning foreign affairs, common to the American experience, have reflected a continuing search for the "real" America.

Only in the shorter term—and only when a clearly categorical opposition exists between the United States and some hostile state on the most fundamental philosophical levels—have Americans en masse suspended their critical instinct and assumed that good intent ensures a good choice of diplomatic methods.[5] In any period of American history, the norm is to discuss method, to sanction dissent even when it is inconvenient, and finally to understand one's actions only as steps toward clear objectives.

To get a reading on recent congressional views, then, entails seeking some sense of the structure in which congressmen and senators cast the issues before them. For one thing, such attention to structure strongly suggests whether Congress is aligned to the enduring baseline characterized by interest in methods and broad goals or to the more tenuous ground of emergency and crisis.

Beneath questions of partisan support and affiliation lies the more significant issue of bipartisanship. When is bipartisanship justified? What costs may fairly be paid in its support? What relationship between domestic political interests and foreign policy interests is correct in the United States? It is, in short, a question of what constitutes "business as usual"?

After World War I, Warren Harding called the country to "normalcy," never criticizing the fact that Americans had rallied in common cause to meet the exigencies of war but certain that the measures taken to meet the emergency must not be extended into American life in time of peace.[6] For current purposes, the question is whether a new normalcy is emerging. Is "usual" to mean an extension of the cold war consensus brought into challenge during the years of war in Vietnam? Or will it return to close examination of the means through which the executive branch and its subordinate agencies operate?

Surveying Congressional Views, 1984

To determine which baseline had the greater currency by 1984, a survey was undertaken to gather from senators and congressmen some expression of their views on a number of major foreign policy and national security issues.[7] The object of the request—which called on each congressional office to forward "what you regard as your representative statements" concerning US policy in Lebanon, El Salvador, and Nicaragua—was to let each office select materials that identified the member's political and policy position and that would be open to analysis.[8] No special request was made that the materials provided indicate the underlying logic of members' concerns or their specific voting positions.

Newsletters sent to home states or districts, standard letters used in response to constituent mail, and extracts of comments made on the floor of the House or Senate constituted much of the material. Less frequently, copies of speeches and radio transcripts were included. These materials could be challenged as thin and rhetorical, yet they remain the language in which Congress communicates with the electorate. Statements designed for constituents' consumption seek to explain and justify positions the congressman or senator is taking. Such materials may thus reveal much about the structure of public discourse on national issues even if they would prove unreliable in predicting the outcome of a vote.[9]

A follow-up letter some two months later thanked those who had already responded, mentioned the types of materials they had sent, and welcomed additional responses and especially first responses from previous nonrespondents. The collection process ended five months after the processing of the first mailing, and the material was entered into a computerized data base.[10] Although the details of the data base of the software and record structure used for its management are important, the issues pertinent here are the questions asked, the implications associated with answers, and the significance attached to various correlations of responses to various questions.[11] Information was also sorted into logical, numerical, and character fields to supplement the study of underlying issues.[12]

A preliminary coding was made according to support or nonsupport of administration policy with respect to each specific case mentioned (Lebanon, El Salvador, and Nicaragua) and to the Middle East and Central America generally. Then the main thrust was to determine the stated or the logically probable reason for either supporting or opposing the policy. Among the critical tests were whether the goals of policy were accepted but not the means, whether the means were seen as potentially acceptable but not the goals, and whether the means matched the chosen goals. If the American experience in Vietnam was specifically mentioned, precisely how it was mentioned and the apparent purpose of doing so were identified if possible. Given the open-endedness of the Vietnam experience, there was a need to determine what specific aspects of it were selected as the relevant "lessons." Particularly because some proponents of administration policies have alleged that references to Vietnam have been the stock in trade of those dissenting from the administration's view, failure to ask more discriminating questions about references to Vietnam would have meant failure to test an unproven allegation. In addition, appropriate character fields for state, party affiliation, and gender were used. Taken together, it was possible to ask such questions as whether those referring to Vietnam typically supported the administration's positions or opposed them; what aspects of the Vietnam experience were seen as lessons suited to current problems; whether endorsements of the administration's views on Vietnam follow party affiliation or other considerations; and whether the congressmen and senators focused on the relationship between the goals of policy and the means employed to achieve them.

Out of a total membership of 535 in both bodies, a total of 146 members of Congress responded. The sampling, which technically does not merit the use of that term, was based exclusively on the senators' and congressmen's willingness to respond. It would have been possible to inspect the *Congressional Record* and other sources in order to have a complete record of all 100 senators and all 435 congressmen, but this would have damaged the data. Some data would have been selected by congressional offices, some chosen from outside. This procedure would also have diminished our view of how senators and congressmen preferred to project themselves on the major issues in foreign and defense affairs. It is not necessary to indulge in overly nice criticism of what senators and congressmen "really mean" by what they say; for present purposes, how they mean to be understood is the key, and this may well be seen in what they say and how they say it. To appreciate the underlying concerns among congressional and other figures, how views are expressed is central. The results presented here are complete with respect to responses received, but they are only partial with respect to the legislature as a whole. They are suggestive rather than final.

Common Ground

Has any common ground emerged in Congress in Vietnam's aftermath? The present inquiry reveals a broad foundation of interrelated ideas, perhaps constituting less a "lesson" of Vietnam than a resurgence of more traditional ideas predating the cold war and made possible by Vietnam's savaging of the cold war consensus. Intense concern appeared over the the means to achieve the stated goals of policy; and blanket acceptance of idealistic pronouncements as statements of policy fell into considerable disrepute. Even if a policy objective appeared desirable, there was more care and scrutiny as to whether the goal was achievable and as to its costs. The penchant for looking at the specifics of implementation rather than just at the broad framework of policy objectives paralleled a renewed assessment of countries in terms of their own histories rather than as part of a global ideological drama.

This focus on concrete means and specific cases was shared by those who supported administration policy and those who opposed it, those who favored a military component in US policy in Central America and those who wished it dramatically reduced, those who emphasized Soviet and Cuban agitation in the region and those who emphasized indigenous sources of conflict. The common ground, then, was insistence on concreteness, on specificity, and on attention to the practical link between measures proposed and effects intended. In addition, a common understanding appeared, a policy pursued without clear support from the American public was in danger from the start. Among congressional respondents to the present inquiry, these ideas took on progressively more specific forms, sometimes supported by careful rationales. Common concerns linking representatives across the political spectrum included the need for clarity in the formulation and statement of national policy, the imperative to define military missions precisely in order to keep them within the originally authorized scope and also to ensure that they were feasible, and the need to convey to the American public both the pertinence of a policy to practical US interests and the likelihood that measures undertaken would have a decent payoff. Blanket explanations evidently lacked appeal and persuasiveness. Commitment of support was more likely when the issue was concrete and the case specific.

The need to make means serve the ends of policy was by far the most pervasive theme. One hundred twenty-six (92.7 percent) of the 146 responding members mentioned the intimate linkage between ends and means of policy. Sixty Republicans and Democrats referring to the dependence of ends on means supported administration policy in Central America, and 66 opposed it. Twenty-one Democrats and Republicans referring to the connection of ends and means and also referring to Vietnam in connection with remarks on Central America favored the administration's actions in the region, and 20 expressed disfavor. The emphasis on how goals are contingent on means, then, was both pervasive and bipartisan.

References to Vietnam were found among those favoring administration policies and those opposing them, as well as among Democrats and Republicans. Seventy-seven respondents favored the administration's policies in Central America, and 69 expressed opposition. Twenty-four respondents referred to Vietnam in reference to Central America and also favored the administration's approach in Central America. Twenty opposed it. Of 45 proadministration respondents, 15 who favored the administration's policies in the Middle East (including Lebanon) cited analogies to Vietnam. This group was proportionally larger than those opposing the administration's handling of Middle Eastern matters and also citing Vietnam.

The strongest undercurrent of concern was to ensure that goals recognized as desirable be sought only by carefully selected means and to make support of those goals conditional on choosing means that had a clear chance of achieving them. When Vietnam was cited, it was largely as a general caution about means and ends. Lessons beyond that were debatable.

The intimate relationship between means and ends was clearly a matter of concern to Congressman Barney Frank (D-Mass.), an opponent of many administration policies. On 27 July 1983, for example, Frank told colleagues in the House, concerning support of the contras in Nicaragua: "If your fundamental purpose is to stop the flow of arms, do not entrust that to people whose fundamental purpose is a different one, whose fundamental purpose understandably is to reclaim their country." Referring to the contras, the Mosquito Indians, and the insurgents under Eden Pastora, Frank said, "They are not in business to help us keep arms out of El Salvador. They are in business to overthrow their own government." Again underscoring that the United States was inevitably limited in its options by the desires of those with whom it worked, Frank concluded: "They are your chosen instruments. Your intentions in this case are less relevant than the stated, and explicit, and perfectly understandable intentions of your chosen instruments."[13]

Frank's manner of analysis and line of argument were extended by Congressman Lawrence J. Smith (D-Fla.). Noting that there were some 10,000 contras under arms at the time, Smith regarded their intentions as obvious from the character of the force and from their public statements. "No one has ever said, from that group, that they are interdicting arms," Smith remarked. "They have never made that claim. Nor would we need, by any military standards, 10,000 men to interdict arms, which is the stated purpose of why they are supposed to be there in the first place."[14]

Congressman Bill Nelson (D-Fla.) said the Vietnam experience had demonstrated that "as a practical matter it is not possible to interdict all of the arms shipment" out of Nicaragua. The underlying insistence on pragmatism—on reasonable conviction that a goal was practically attainable—fit into the general "lesson" learned from Vietnam.[15]

Proponents of administration policy also professed concern to find the most suitable means of seeking national goals. Although "Vietnam taught us to think twice before getting involved in the affairs of other nations," as Congressman Richard Cheney (R-Wyo.) wrote in a newsletter for his constituents in November 1983, there remained affairs originating in other nations' problems that still involved US interests and could involve US intervention in some form. Although seeking to avoid "getting sucked into *their* military conflicts," it remained true that *our* interests sometimes rode upon the outcome of *their* disputes.[16] Caution was justified, but automatic avoidance of involvement was not.

Congressman Gerry E. Studds (D-Mass.) considered US policies inapt to their contexts. Studds likened efforts by State Department representatives to demonstrate that the situation in El Salvador and Central America generally was improving to "State and Defense Department briefings during the Vietnam War, when Congress was always told that just a little more money and just a few more thousand soldiers would get the job done."[17] This observation, provoked by consideration of the Kissinger Commission's report on Central American affairs, seems to have been rooted in the same essential assumptions as Studds's March 1981 report to the House Committee on Foreign Affairs (Central America, 1981). "If there is any lesson to be learned from Vietnam and from the history of US relations with Latin America," Studds then concluded, "it is that good intentions are not sufficient to make good policy."[18] A goal of the highest esteem could not substitute for a persuasive and effective pattern of means suited to the goal's accomplishment.

But "no more Vietnams" did not have to mean avoiding involvements when they held the prospect of having a military dimension. It could mean instead an avoidance of false steps and failed strategy, much as the Eisenhower administration sought to use the phrase "no more Koreas" not to suggest anything remotely approaching isolation but only to proclaim that Truman's way of handling the conflict on the Korean peninsula would not be repeated by his successor. Speaking in support of Reagan administration policy in Central America, Congressman Sam B. Hall, Jr. (D-Tex.), expressed his belief that "a large percentage of the American people remain skeptical over *any* involvement by the United States in Central America," even allowing that it was an understandable attitude given the difficulties experienced in Vietnam.[19] Hall advocated handling Central American difficulties by means and scenarios different from those that unfolded in Vietnam. In the end, "no more Vietnams" could be a caution against committing an error more than against making a commitment at all.

The attention to precisely how a measure was supposed to achieve its announced result also showed itself clearly and frequently in discussions of US policy in Lebanon. It was not only a question of what the United States wished to achieve through its actions but also what results it could reasonably expect. Congressman Richard Ray of Georgia, who thought that the administration never clearly articulated a mission for US Marines in Lebanon, emphasized that "not enough thought was given to the possible consequences of military involvement before that involvement was undertaken."[20] For present purposes, it is less critical to judge the administration's policy than to appreciate the mechanism of evaluation implicit in the congressman's comment. Reaction to the immediately apparent problem would not suffice; a reasonable estimate of the aggregate commitment over the long run was essential, as was a comparable forecast of likely effects of US actions. A simple version might read, "The United States had better know what it's getting into and know what getting into it can actually accomplish." Generalities could be voiced easily but attained only with difficulty; and a general objective could be stated even with no clear means to realize the objective. As Senator Thomas Eagleton (D-Mo.) put it, "Peace-keeping is an amorphous phase, not an assigned military mission."[21] Congressman Henry Waxman (D-Calif.) referred to the mission of the US Marines in Lebanon as "indefinable."[22] The term *peace-keeping* seemed to such observers more a generalized goal than a specific means to a desired outcome. Endorsing such a broad goal, whether characterized as an "amorphous phase" or not, seemed like giving the executive a blank check.

Consistent with this logic was a reference that Congressman Charles E. Bennett of Florida made in the House on 28 September 1983 to the Gulf of Tonkin Resolution. Calling it the one vote out of some 15,000 he had cast as a congressman that he would take back if he had the opportunity, Bennett did not merely raise the "specter" of "another Vietnam." He objected to the blanket authorization by Congress of presidential discretionary action. He reminded the House that he had voted against the War Powers Act on grounds that "it improperly gave power to the president."[23] In short, the operative concern was in the manner of doing business—in its constitutionality and in its prudential deliberateness—and not in an ill-conceived assumption that the Vietnam scenario was waiting in the wings to be replayed.

The focus on how means are expected to achieve the desired goals of policy proved especially sharp in "Key Lessons of the United States Involvement in Lebanon," an essay by Congressman Ike Skelton of Missouri. Allowing that the first deployment of Marines in the summer of 1982 made sense because it had a "valid military mission" of overseeing the withdrawal of PLO forces from Beirut, Skelton disputed the wisdom of a second deployment after the assassination of President Bashir Gemayel. Citing President Reagan's explanation that the new deployment would "facilitate the restoration of Lebanese sovereignty," Skelton styled the mission as "essentially diplomatic." "How such force was to help back up the effort was not really very clear," he added. The deployment seemed, in other words, too imprecise in purpose for its mission to be stated at all.

Skelton also noted that neither Robert McFarlane nor Donald Rumsfeld were Middle East experts, nor were they professional diplomats. "While all three men are extremely capable individuals," he added, "the President could have appointed others more qualified for the specific task at hand."[24] In short, if US forces were to be used properly, the real question was not whether the United States had an interest in the region but what particular steps would really serve US interests and in what ways they would do so. This was not merely a corrective to what Skelton saw as deficiencies in the administration's approach but also a caution to Congress and to the American public. Suggesting that the "wound" of Vietnam had yet to heal completely, Skelton said Americans were uneasy about putting troops on the ground "in unstable areas of the world." But the handling of an overseas problem must not be warped by such uneasiness. "The problem with the decision to deploy forces in Lebanon," Skelton noted, "was that we hoped to show our 'commitment' to the government of President Gemayel on the cheap."[25]

Congressman John McCain (R-Ariz.), customarily sympathetic to the administration's views, nonetheless rose in opposition during House debate on the Multinational Force in Lebanon Resolution to authorize the presence of US forces there under the War Powers Act. McCain specifically referred to the prerequisites for a US military involvement offered by Gen Maxwell Taylor shortly after the Indochina conflict. Those requirements—clearly explainable objectives, clear support of the president by Congress, reasonable expectation of success, and support of our objectives from our allies—had not been met, according to Congressman McCain; and, in this sense, lessons learned through the Vietnam experience suggested reason to pause.[26]

It was not the prospect of involvement itself that invited comparisons between Vietnam and Lebanon or Central America for Senator David Durenberger (R-Minn.). What Durenberger found "eerily reminiscent of the final stages of the Vietnam War" when he assessed the situation in Lebanon as of 30 January 1984 was a simultaneous unwillingness to take those steps necessary to obtain a "decisive battlefield victory," an uncertainty as to what political purpose such a victory would serve, and insistence that US troops nonetheless stay at least long enough to preserve US "credibility" while "we accomplished a face-saving withdrawal."[27] Durenberger also compared Central America to Southeast Asia in various respects, seeing the former as "haunted by the memories of Vietnam." Yet Durenberger noted pointedly that what those memories meant varied widely, suggesting to some that "we should never again involve ourselves in foreign policy unless it is on the side of the angels." Others thought that "we must somehow restore our credibility as a superpower."[28] It was not necessarily specific places that troubled Durenberger; nor was such high policy necessarily where he himself saw potentially dangerous similarities with the Vietnam experience. It was instead "the manner by which we seem to be approaching our policy ..., and it is this parallel, I believe, which bears closer attention."[29] What Durenberger insisted on was a Central American policy rooted in the realities of Central America—not driven by visions falsely harbored from the days of Vietnam.

Senator Durenberger cautioned that US policy in Central America was "haunted" by memories of Vietnam that encouraged an extreme stance, whether to avoid involvement or to demonstrate US status as a persuasive superpower. But for Durenberger, the lessons of Vietnam were perhaps most usefully those about "the making of policy." The superficial similarities between Vietnam and El Salvador, for example, ought to be appreciated for their limits; and the specific military and practical lessons should be learned—that sustaining operations in El Salvador might be easier than doing so in Vietnam, that the "much-maligned domino theory" was not bankrupt, that guerrillas can be beaten, and the like. But the central issue, as Durenberger saw it, was that "we made and sustained a broad and open-ended commitment, enshrined that commitment in terms of a large doctrine, and thereafter were forced to live bound up in a number of dilemmas." Durenberger suggested that it had not been the level of violence in Vietnam that had determined the degree of US commitment but, rather, that US commitment had itself driven up the intensity of the war. The deepest problems with the pursuit of policy and the prosecution of the war in Vietnam stemmed from US adherence to contradictory propositions: "First, do not lose another country to communism. Second, do not fight a land war in Asia. These two unstated rules, contradictory as they were, forced us into the policy of incrementalism which ultimately spelled our failure." The important lesson to be carried from the Vietnam experience into the pursuit of policy in El Salvador was to match "our will and our resources to the stakes allegedly involved." Anything short of that "promises disaster." For Durenberger, it was the discrepancy between broad proclamations that US national interest was at stake and US professions that it would avoid commitment of combat forces which was really "calling forth memories in Vietnam."[30] Specificity, concreteness, feasibility—such were the criteria of judgment and concern forming a broad common ground in Congress a decade after Vietnam.

A corollary of the insistence that actions of the US government be appropriate to the situation was the assertion of a criterion for appropriateness. The key to congressional determination of a suitable standard was enhanced emphasis on the distinctive historical development of each country and region in which the United States might be a player. Members from both congressional bodies and both parties commented on the need to understand each problem, each country, and each region on its own terms.[31]

This concern extended to those enthusiastic about current policies and to those skeptical of them. Congressman Don Bonker (D-Wash.) warned on 28 July 1983 that the United States risked serious error in its Central American policy, "once again . . . forming policies along East-West lines not unlike the 1960s and our deepening entanglement in Southeast Asia." The lesson of Vietnam that clearly affected Congressman Bonker was the danger in using a "blanket" explanation of policy in place of a more detailed delineation of how specific measures suited US interests in the circumstances of many different nations. Congressman Bonker urged "the removal of the conflict in Central America from the context of East-West confrontation," thus focusing on the needs and conditions of Central America itself rather than on a bipolar global confrontation.[32]

Senator George Mitchell (D-Maine) sought to distinguish between Vietnam and current problem areas. In comments on a supplemental aid bill for El Salvador on 5 April 1984, he warned that "the debate over El Salvador shows every sign of turning into a national referendum on Vietnam." Although a critic of administration policy in the region, Mitchell expressed his hope that such a linkage not develop "because the differences between El Salvador and Vietnam are far more important than the superficial similarities."[33] Mitchell cited the comparative proximity of El Salvador to US territory as compared to the 9,000-mile remove of Vietnam, much as supporters of the administration cited it. Mitchell also referred to the need to keep the Panama Canal secure, as proponents of administration policy did. And Mitchell acknowledged that the Soviet Union and Cuba contributed to unrest in Central America but he gave far greater emphasis to the indigenous causes for the unrest. Mitchell noted, for example, that US involvement in Vietnam was an extension of Vietnam's struggle to end the colonization most recently exercised by the Japanese and the French while El Salvador's colonial status had ended in 1821. These different histories led to different sets of problems, different requirements for their solution, and different understandings of how much and what kind of aid an outside that Mitchell believed had pertinence to the debate over El Salvador was what he called "the apparent unwillingness of the administration to recognize that each country had its own history, its own culture, its own economic relationships, and its own legacy of friendships and animosities."[34] For Mitchell, then, it was not right to make blanket comparisons between Vietnam and El Salvador at all; but it was important to adjust the American mentality—the mechanisms, logic, and framework by which US officials understood the world around them.

One supporter of administration policy in Central America who accepted the need for a military component in US involvement in the region pointed toward Vietnam's potential as a "value-free" or nonpartisan source of guidance. The message of the Southeast Asian experience was not isolation but investigation. Congressman Cheney of Wyoming wrote to his constituents: "Vietnam taught us to think twice before again getting involved in the affairs of other nations...."[35] Although some might, after that second thought, choose to avoid involvement in Central America, Cheney was not among them; nor did the mere fact of taking a second look require any close comparisons to the specific details of the Vietnam scenario. The issue, as Cheney saw it, was not to ask whether El Salvador was like Vietnam. It was to ask what was happening in El Salvador, what the implications were for US interests, what those US interests really were, and what measures showed any actual prospect for being effective. What "Vietnam taught us," then, was not a specific course of action to be followed but a checklist of concerns to be kept in mind.

Congressman Bill Nelson (D-Fla.), in a release dated 29 July 1983, tried to illustrate how a lesson drawn from the relatively unproductive enterprise in Vietnam could be used to support administration policy in other areas, specifically an operation that bore some limited similarities to the one in Vietnam. Nelson favored US support of Nicaraguan contras as a means of interdicting arms shipments, noting that it would be impossible to cut completely the flow of arms from Nicaragua to El Salvador. "We learned that lesson in Vietnam," Nelson observed.[36] The consequence of that lesson for present policy, however, was not to avoid the attempt but to temper one's expectations as to its predictable results. Recalling Vietnam did not require avoidance of the general kind of operation that may have been conducted there, although it did invite an effort to identify difficulties in Vietnam and to deal with matters in current trouble spots on their own terms.

Across a wide spectrum of opinion on what should actually be done in Central America, there was a shared emphasis on the importance of tailoring any US involvement to each country and to the region as a whole. As Congressman Richard H. Lehman (D-Calif.) put it, "The solution that is finally arrived at must be compatible with Central America's needs and history, not simply our own...."[37] That the United States might need to history, not simply our own. . . ."³⁷ That the United States might need to bow—or least nod—to the internal determinants of a region or country became a more acceptable attitude after Vietnam.

Whatever specific appraisal congressmen made of the administration's policies, they strongly urged that policies be shaped and carried out only within the tolerances of the American public. Perhaps the best synthesis of views in the Congress was represented by the words of Congressman Jim Slattery (D-Kans.): "While I resist attempts to equate Central America with Vietnam, I recognize that conditions in Central America are clouded for many of us because of our memories of the Vietnam War."³⁸ Noting that popular support for US military involvement in Central America was lacking, Slattery said, "We must be sure that Americans firmly support each action."³⁹ In this criterion, he differed little from high-ranking officers in the Army and the other services. Vietnam was neither a blanket explanation of the world nor a set of specific lessons to be applied in every trouble spot. It was an inducement to determine the means by which desirable goals might realistically be pursued. As vague as Vietnam's supposed lessons were, the impact of Vietnam was to foster attention to the specific.

Senator Alan Cranston (D-Calif.) expressed concerns closely resembling those of high-ranking US military officers as to the circumstances under which national security policies could be pursued. "One of the key lessons of Vietnam," Cranston suggested in the Senate on 1 March 1983, was that "support of the American people is vital for the success of our foreign policy."⁴⁰ Similarly, when questioning the course of administration policy in Lebanon, Cranston emphasized that a war so costly and complex as that in Vietnam had been fought without unity and popular support in the United States and only with "trauma and controversy and division within our country."⁴¹ Clearly, then, a key question was whether US policy *toward* Vietnam had been derived from circumstances *within* Vietnam.

The Distinctiveness of Proadministration Viewpoints

The shared concern that abstraction was dangerous still allowed for a wide range of disagreement on specific policies. On the whole, those tending to favor the administration's actions in overseas trouble spots also emphasized threats to security. In Central America and also in the Middle East, they cited Cuba and the Soviet Union as sources of agitation and unrest. They were more likely to make analogies to Vietnam when discussing the risks to US security in Central America. In comparing Vietnam with Central America, supporters of the administration typically focused on the potential damage the United States would sustain by failing to achieve a stated goal. In this light, "Vietnam" cautioned against a strong hostile concentration at comparatively close quarters. It meant the specter of refugees fleeing revolution and insurgency—and having no ocean barriers to control the numbers streaming across US borders. The sense of crisis was real and keen.

In general, respondents sympathetic to the administration's policies in Central America and elsewhere were significantly more likely to cite the Soviet Union and Cuba as contributors to unrest and crisis, or even as the main causes, than were those dissenting from the administration's views. Seventy-seven (52.7 percent) respondents expressed agreement with US policies in Central America, 65 of them warning that national security was at stake in the region and specifically citing the Soviet Union and Cuba. Many of these respondents mentioned the need for linking ends and means, but they placed even greater emphasis on what they perceived to be the nonindigenous aspects of the region's unrest. They also tended to see the problems of Central America as part of a global confrontation between the United States and the Soviet Union. One-third of those who favored US policies in the area also cited the Soviet Union and Cuba as sources of general threat to US security and referred to Vietnam to support their positions. Only one proadministration congressman made reference to Vietnam without explicitly naming the Soviet Union or Cuba as at least a contributor to the regional unrest.

Only 13 of the 69 respondents unsympathetic to the US government's actions in Central America also explicitly discussed the relationship of US national security to the outcome of events in the area. In fact, proadministration members of Congress were as likely to cite Vietnam as were members on the other side of the issue. Only 16 nonsupporters who did not mention the area's connection to US security interests referred to Vietnam in explaining Central America. Forty of the 69 did not cite Vietnam or the security issue at all, concentrating on what they perceived to be a problem in the relationship of means and ends. Emphasis on the relationship of local and regional problems to transcendent issues of global security appeared to be more significant than reference to Vietnam.

Similar views emerged over US relations with other countries in Central America and the Middle East. On structural questions, such as how to determine when to make a commitment, there was broad agreement without regard to party affiliation or one's interpretation of Vietnam. On determining whether US interests were concretely threatened in a particular situation, the inclination ran high to see Soviet and Cuban involvement rather than indigenous forces as the main criterion of endangerment. Forty-nine (63.6 percent) of those supporting the administration on Central American matters pointedly blamed the USSR, Cuba, or both, while only 10 (14.5 percent) of those opposing the US position in the region made reference to either the USSR or Cuba.

In general, congressional respondents who supported existing administration policies were far more likely to relate potential problems in immigration to heightened national security vulnerability. Eleven (14.3 percent) proadministration respondents cited the immigration problem (10 of these also explicitly associated it with Vietnam) while only 2 (2.9 percent) opponents of administration policy did so (neither referred to Vietnam). Sixty-five (84.4 percent) of those respondents favoring the administration in the area cited the threat to national security (23, or 29.9 percent, of these also referred to Vietnam) while only 13 of those differing with the administration cited national security (only 4, or 5.8 percent, of these referred to Vietnam).

In attaching a specific set of meanings to the generalized notion of Vietnam, one group focused on external sources for problems emerging in various countries. The alternative group concentrated more on internal origins of problems in each locality and region.

Congressman Richard Shelby (D-Ala.), a strong proponent of the administration's policies toward Central America, charged in a mailing to constituents: "Opponents of the president constantly resurrect the ghost of Vietnam when criticizing the administration's policies. . . . Central America, however, is not Vietnam." He cited the Panama Canal, a potential direct threat to the US southern flank, and a nearby "haven for revolutionaries" on our doorstep as crucial differences. "Raising the specter of 'another Vietnam' provides convenient cover for dereliction of duty," he asserted. At the same time, however, Shelby made an apparent oblique reference to the influx of the "boat people" fleeing from Southeast Asia after the fall of the South Vietnamese regime and perhaps those leaving Cuba and Haiti as well, warning of millions of "foot people" fleeing Communist governments in El Salvador, Honduras, and even Mexico, and of "our borders being overrun by millions of hungry refugees who only desire to live in peace."[42] The "ghost of Vietnam," it would seem, could walk in both directions, haunting some with memories of confusing policies and confused execution while visiting others with nightmares of fallen dominoes and burdensome refugees.

Congressman William L. "Bill" Dickinson (R-Ala.), customarily supportive of administration policy on the use of armed force, also pointed to the prospect of "additional hundreds of thousands of refugees" who would flee countries such as El Salvador in the event of a takeover by Communist forces. He referred to the refugee problems in Southeast Asia, Cuba, and Nicaragua as precedent; and he judged efforts to prevent a new flood of refugees as justified "from a moral and humane perspective, and our own self-interest. . . ."[43] Congressman Thomas N. Kindness (R-Ohio), substantially supporting existing US government policies in Central America in his August-September 1983 constituent newsletter, distinguished the present problem from the experience in Vietnam. "Unlike our involvement in Vietnam, we have clearly defined objective and interest." In addition, he emphasized that the effects of a US withdrawal or abstention from aid should be considered: "If we learned anything from the Vietnam War, it should be that bloodbaths follow Communist takeovers. Hundreds of thousands of boat people drowned in an attempt to flee the concentration camps and firing squads. When we talk about 'another Vietnam,' that's the kind of bloodletting we're talking about...."[44]

Senator Pete Wilson (R-Calif.) said, "Central America need not become another Vietnam," but what he meant was that the Central American states need not fall to Marxist insurgencies. He worried that the United States might interpose itself in the region's affairs with damaging effect if it bought time for either insurgents or the Sandinista government in Nicaragua, warning of "the same result which a US-negotiated 'peace' brought to South Vietnam and Cambodia."[45]

Congressman Thomas F. Hartnett (R-S.C.) argued from the apparent effects of a cutoff in economic and military aid to South Vietnam in 1975 that Congress should support aid to the existing governments in Central America in the 1980s to prevent new governments hostile to the United States from taking power. The effects Hartnett imputed from refusal to authorize the $700 million that Gerald Ford requested in 1975 were "three million murders" in Cambodia, the extinction of human rights in Vietnam, and the domination of Cambodia and Laos by Vietnam while it continued "picking away" at Thailand. For Hartnett, such unpleasant results were the real "folly of Vietnam," as well as the basis of the central lesson to be learned.[46]

Criticizing what he styled "the isolationist strains in our thinking," Congressman Jim Courter (R-N.J.) called for a different view. In a commencement address to the Admiral Farragut Academy in Toms River, New Jersey, on 4 June 1983, Courter emphasized the need for US involvement in world affairs even though that could sometimes lead to a decision to use military force. The Vietnam experience, in his view, justified such an approach. "After the war," he said, "bloodbaths occurred. Cambodia fell like a domino and a holocaust occurred there. Countless Vietnamese risked their lives in small boats to flee communism, and many died on the high seas." Seeing no hope for democracy in the areas under Hanoi's control, Courter linked moral and strategic interests, and he criticized reluctance to intervene in Central America as "[hiding] our head in the sand when the going gets tough."[47] Memories of Vietnam clearly lingered; but, just as clearly, they did not mandate rejection of military or other involvement.

The prospects of immigrants flooding across the southern border of the United States greatly concerned some in Congress. Congressman James V. Hansen (R-Utah) warned his correspondents that "one half million boat people came to the US after the Marxist-Leninists triumphed in Vietnam" and that "many Latins will flee that tyranny" if it is installed in Central America.[48] Congressman Robert J. Lagomarsino (R-Calif.) also cited the prospect of immigrants as a compelling issue whose gravity could be understood through the example of Vietnam. In his summer 1983 circular, "US Policy in Central America," Lagomarsino repeated the estimate of "two to seven million 'foot people'" coming to the United States. "The economic and social costs of the Vietnamese boat people were overwhelming," he said, and a much larger influx of immigrants would constitute a "strain on US security."[49]

Even when dissenting somewhat from some specific aspects of administration policy concerning Nicaragua or El Salvador, some members of Congress explicitly agreed with the most unqualified proadministration spokesmen as to the importance of Central America for US strategic security. They shunned comparison of El Salvador with Vietnam. Congressman Robin Britt (D-N.C.), for example, thought that "we must avoid the temptation to view El Salvador merely as another Vietnam. El Salvador is of vital importance to our national interest due to its close proximity to our borders," he added, "unlike Vietnam, which was thousands of miles away." In addition, Britt said El Salvador had "a democratic government elected in open elections" that should be supported and encouraged.[50] Perhaps the fundamental difference he saw between the situations in El Salvador and in Vietnam was that El Salvador's comparative proximity to the United States posed a greater threat to US security.

Congressman Shelby complained that opponents of administration policy in Central America "constantly resurrect the ghost of Vietnam"; but at the same time, he used it to explain the importance of Central America. The stake for US security in Central America clearly impressed Shelby, who noted that Vietnam did not "sit astride our Panama Canal lifeline" or "provide a haven for revolutionaries to gleefully perch on our doorstep." Raising "the specter of [another Vietnam]" when US interests hinged on the outcome of Central American developments struck Shelby as a "convenient cover for dereliction of duty."[51] Congressman Dan Schaefer (R-Colo.) similarly wrote that discussion of "our presence in Lebanon showed the people's willingness to link any involvement abroad with the experience of the Vietnam era."[52] Congressman Sam Hall (D-Tex.) focused on the proximity of Central American nations to the United States. The potential impact on US security of unfavorable outcomes in the region should discourage a simplistic reliance on "the expression [no more Vietnams]" in charting US policy.[53]

Some congressmen who explicitly referred to Vietnam in constituent mail did so to deny connections between the experience in Vietnam and the present circumstances in Central America. Congressman Larry E. Craig (R-Idaho) styled it "an exercise in political drum-beating."[54] Craig denied that the insurgency in El Salvador was a civil war, seeing the armed insurgents there as players in an "ideological conflict" to which Cuba and the Soviet

Union were parties.[55] If it was an insurgency rather than a civil war, then US involvement was justified to enhance US national security.

Senator Jeremiah Denton (R-Ala.), a supporter of administration policy in Central America and elsewhere, observed on 8 March 1984 that the United States had been hampered in its foreign policy efforts by the impact of Vietnam. "Since Vietnam," he said, "we have been defeated in every foreign policy issue of major importance confronting this Nation because of . . . disunity. The Redskins could not beat Vassar that way, and we did not beat a little country called North Vietnam because of the same insane lack of bipartisanship of a common purpose of serving the interests of this Nation."[56] Denton believed that the Vietnam experience had made potential adversaries think the United States could not defend its interests. He even attributed the 1973 increase in oil prices to a belief that the United States would not act.[57] Bipartisanship in foreign affairs remained the watchword of those concerned over support for the president. They passionately objected to Soviet and Cuban interventionism, and they worried about refugees and other consequences of instability.

Sources of Skepticism

Vietnam has been used to challenge administration policies, but the term "using Vietnam" is not meaningful in itself. The open-endedness, flexibility, and ambiguity of the Vietnam experience make it like the proverbial "picture worth a thousand words." Each person referring to Vietnam picks one or another of the thousand words, perhaps changing his choices as situations change.

What was distinctive about those who opposed administration policies in the early 1980s? And what importance did their special emphasis have for the US military? A clue lies in the frequency of reference to the War Powers Act of 1975, especially when linked to the frequency with which the Soviet Union or Cuba are cited as sources of local or regional problems and to the degree of attention cast on the dependence of US national security on the outcome of various regional difficulties. The number of congressional respondents explicitly referring to the War Powers Act was small, but most of those who did were out of sympathy with existing US policies toward Central America and Lebanon. Eleven of the 13 (84.6 percent) respondents referring to the War Powers Act opposed the administration on Central American matters, and 12 (92.3 percent) opposed the handling of US involvement in Lebanon. Only three (23.1 percent) respondents specifically mentioning the War Powers Act cited the Soviet Union and Cuba as sources of problems in either region, and only one of these did so in favor of administration policy in both areas. None of the

11 dissenters from existing policies on Central America specifically mentioned the Soviet Union or Cuba.

One could infer that the underlying concern of those citing the War Powers Act was related to constitutional questions about the balance of power between Congress and the president rather than external threats. Even so, those citing the War Powers Act were also concerned over outside parties becoming engaged in local and regional problems; and those who emphasized the Soviet or Cuban part in Central American affairs shared the concern over constitutional issues. The difference was quite possibly a matter of balance and emphasis.

The War Powers Act did not specify that the United States avoid overseas conflict but rather that the commitments be made case-by-case and be sustained by agreement between the president and Congress. Opponents of the administration's foreign policies in the early 1980s dissented from the view that world politics was essentially bipolar. Departing from cold war globalism, they focused on local circumstances to make sense out of regional and local problems, playing down the US-Soviet relationship. They particularly criticized the methods for making and executing US policy. Their references to Vietnam focused on how the enterprise was conducted and not on how it turned out.

Although both Republicans and Democrats were among the critics of US policy on Central America and Lebanon, some Democratic members of Congress were clearly more visible. Congressman Henry B. Gonzalez (D-Tex.), for example, prepared a column for the *San Antonio Light* dated 11 March 1984 in which he styled administration policy toward El Salvador as "simply to support a Vietnam-like war." Describing the government in Managua as "not even up to the standard of being wretched," he saw the guerrillas as "winning a stalemate." Charging that local governments in Central America suffered from corruption that was "routine and endemic," he concluded that "Central America today is a vivid reminder of Vietnam" and that the practices of those governments simply strengthened the guerrillas.[58]

Congressman Gerry E. Studds (D-Mass.) agreed, comparing briefings on conditions in Lebanon in the 1980s to those given on Vietnam in the 1960s: "Congress was always told that just a little more money and just a few more thousand soldiers would get the job done."[59] Studds and other congressmen sent letters to their colleagues in the House criticizing US policy on Central America. They said a US presence made Honduras look less like an independent country than like "a clone for the early days in Saigon."[60]

Still, even when skepticism approached cynicism, how Vietnam was handled clearly surpassed the outcome of the conflict as the key concern. On 4 April 1984, for example, Senator Joseph R. Biden, Jr., of Delaware cited Vietnam while expressing doubt that progress in training El Salvadoran

USAF AFTER VIETNAM

government forces was significant: "We have been told by the military time and again that this training process is really moving along—'Vietnamization is really working. We are really on our way. It is really going to work.'"[61] "[Some] of us cynics from the Vietnam age," Biden noted, "are reminded of similar things we were told about how Americans were not involved, about how we were only training, but how gradually and gradually and gradually our presence built up."[62] The argument went beyond comparing physical circumstances; it touched on the fundamental credibility and trustworthiness of policymakers and their principal agents.

Sounding a cautionary note of US policy in Central America and calling for reexamination of specific measures supported by US agencies, Senator Daniel K. Inouye (D-Hawaii) took a more subdued tone. His concern focused on the thinking of US policymakers. Specifically, Inouye noted that limited measures taken gradually had added up to a major commitment even without full study of a "path we followed blindly" in the 1960s, one which "led inexorably to American combat involvement."[63] Superficial similarities were not the problem, and Inouye recognized differences in the societies involved and in geography. It was the need to examine the cumulative impact of seemingly limited measures that most concerned Inouye. Unwilling to dismiss the "domino theory" out of hand, he alleged that visions of Vietnam were greater among advocates of continued military commitments to Central American countries. "They look toward Central America and the demands for a negotiated end to the bloodletting," he wrote, "and they see Laos; ... they hear the ominous echo—Vietnam." For him, the broad lessons of Vietnam had more to do with how the United States acted than with how other nations acted toward the United States. Inouye concluded that it was the administration which was fighting "the battles of the past."[64]

This discussion of methods lay at the heart of understanding goals. Indeed, methods sometimes seemed to be the litmus test of what one's goals really were. For those skeptical of the US role in some trouble areas after the mid-1970s, Vietnam pointed to the impossibility of separating means from ends. Congressman Leon Panetta of California, for example, said it was "of utmost importance that we not forget the lessons of Vietnam" when dealing with problems in El Salvador. "The prospects for victory on the battlefield will remain elusive as long as the guerrillas can continue to draw support from the Salvadoran people."[65] Recognizing that some kind of military component to US involvement might be inevitable, he insisted that the United States "recognize the limits of military force in resolving the many complex problems in the region...."[66] It was not a question of whether force was wrong in itself—the question was whether force was relevant to the specific situation.

Congress and the Military: Politics, Threat, and "Normalcy"

It is true that many congressmen and others skeptical of administration foreign policy did exploit the experience of Vietnam; but so did supporters of the administration. Although critics may have cited Vietnam more often, it was not to call for isolation. Instead, references to Vietnam from either faction suggested the reappearance of a traditional dichotomy in American political life. To speak of "politics" is not to deprecate the process, since it merely means the public's business; and to speak of dichotomy is to suggest neither disloyalty nor impropriety, since polarities grow naturally in nonauthoritarian societies.

But serious problems in communication have often arisen whenever the US Congress and the nation's military services have viewed the world from widely divergent perspectives. The consequences of confusion can be serious, since the practical work of the military depends on funding. Force structure and strategy should ideally follow policy. Although the military must take its lead from the executive department, its credibility also depends on communicating with Congress and with many nongovernmental parties. What has occurred in the past when criteria used by the military have differed from those of Congress? What has resulted when the military services have presented their budget request and other proposals based on a false vision of prevailing congressional views? Could strategic force structure generate enthusiasm in a Congress interested in flexible response at varying levels? If a service argued that forces designed to meet military emergencies would also serve effectively in prolonged low-intensity conflicts, would Congress sense a conflict between ends and means? Many more questions could be phrased; but the ultimate one is whether Congress, the president, and the military can stay tuned to the same wavelength.

The resurgent interest among civilians in means and the goals they serve may have marked the beginnings of a renaissance of trust in professional military judgment. Having goals is an enshrined principle open to common sense, but determining whether goals are attainable and relevant may require trained, skilled, and professional judgment.

The observation that US military officers have often been wary about military commitments also fosters a readiness to look at the details of military programs. It received additional support from Senator Gary Hart (D-Colo.) who, in criticizing what he described as "alarming plans to increase sharply the American military presence in Central America," cited midlevel military officers who had expressed "serious reservations about the direction of our Central American policy."[67] The very fact of using such references suggests the compatibility between a focus on matching means with ends and a positive regard for the views of military professionals.

It is not imperative that the military services take a "worst-case" view of the world. But the need to calculate real threats of hostilities may predispose military personnel in favor of urgency or crisis. Congressional views were predisposed in the same direction during the era of cold war consensus. The question yet unanswered is how satisfactory a readjustment will come as military professionals and political representatives realign in more traditional ways and leave behind them the atypical alignments of the cold war era.

The Vietnam War broke the bipartisan consensus on security and foreign policy matters that had prevailed through the height of the cold war. It may also have taken away much of the general attitude, supposition, and inclination on which the consensus depended. The quest for a bipartisan approach in the 1980s and beyond could be jeopardized by assuming that only one set of assumptions prevailed. If different factions pressed competing sets of assumptions and inclinations, each seeing itself as the essence of "normalcy," confusion could become normal.

Notes

1. Discussions of the cold war era abound. A useful commentary on the distinctive impact of the cold war on US policy and, indeed, on American history is Lloyd C. Gardner, "The Cold War in History," in Gardner, *Architects of Illusion* (Chicago: Quadrangle Books, 1970). On the perceived need for subordination of group or class issues to a "national consensus on turning back the Soviets' economic challenge" during the Kennedy administration, see Bruce Miroff, *Pragmatic Illusions* (New York: David McKay Company, Inc., 1976), 169-72. The need for reasoned dissent from the official, consensus view on policy is a key theme in J. William Fulbright, *The Arrogance of Power* (New York: Vintage Books, 1966), while the "strategy of consensus" is specifically lauded in Lyndon B. Johnson, *The Vantage Point* (London: Widenfeld and Nicolson, 1971), 29-32. Although Johnson emphasizes the need for rallying after the assassination of John F. Kennedy, the impulse toward consensus clearly extended to foreign affairs as well as domestic matters.

2. On various aspects of the conflict between Federalists and Jeffersonian Republicans and on the underlying differences in philosophical approach, see Richard H. Kohn, *Eagle and Sword* (New York: Free Press, 1975). The linkage of domestic policy and what directions the development of the United States should take with the nature of US foreign and defense policy showed itself clearly in the "quasi-war" with France in 1798-1800. Howard P. Nash, Jr., *The Forgotten Wars* (New York: A. S. Barnes, 1968); and Gardner W. Allen, *Our Naval War with France* (Boston: Houghton Mifflin, 1909). Similar differences lurked behind the alternative notions of Federalists and Jeffersonian Republicans during the War of 1812. Probably the best single volume on the war is John K. Mahon, *The War of 1812* (Chicago: University of Chicago Press, 1965), although most major commentaries on the Federalist-Republican clash appear in diplomatic histories, such as Julius W. Pratt, *The Expansionists of 1812* (New York: P. Smith, 1949 [1925]). On the Federalist-Republican clash as a matter of military theory, see Russell F. Weigley, *The American Way of War* (New York: Macmillan Publishing Co., Inc., 1973), 40-55.

3. Concerning alternatives in the era of the Mexican War, a useful introduction is Frederick Merk, *Manifest Destiny and Mission in American History* (New York: Knopf, 1963).

4. Robert L. Beisner, *Twelve against Empire: The Anti-Imperialists 1898-1900* (New York: McGraw-Hill, 1968); and Julius W. Pratt, *The Expansionists of 1898* (Baltimore: Johns Hopkins University Press, 1936).

5. The present argument accepts the notion that "checks and balances" applies not only to domestic political matters but to foreign affairs as well, although the mechanisms for exerting it are not the same in both spheres. The tradition of "checks and balances" within the US military itself is well established, although it is rarely brought out for scrutiny and public attention. The preservation of militia and national guard units in the nineteenth century, even while the regular forces were enhanced, was deliberate. The belief was that federal and state interests varied sufficiently to support different, though not necessarily competing, purposes. Even the arguments used during the military reorganization after World War II owed much to the notion of checks and balances.

6. The fact that the change in policy after World War I did not constitute isolation but rather a return to traditional emphasis in military affairs emerges clearly in Edward M. Coffman, *The Hilt of the Sword* (Madison: University of Wisconsin Press, 1966); and Daniel R. Beaver, *Newton D. Baker and the American War Effort, 1917-1919* (Lincoln: University of Nebraska Press, 1966).

7. The survey was undertaken specifically for this study under sponsorship of the Airpower Research Institute, Center for Aerospace Doctrine, Research, and Education. As is customary, the requests forwarded to Congress were first sent to the local Public Affairs Office; and copies were also forwarded to Legislative Liaison at the Pentagon for information. The requests occasioned no objections.

8. See appendix A for a copy of the initial inquiry.

9. The whole matter of how to assess material, especially along the lines suggested here, involves some considerations of theory. Basically, the manner of argument used here depends on "structuralism" such as has been pioneered by Claude Levi-Strauss. See, for example, Levi-Strauss, *The Savage Mind* (Chicago: University of Chicago Press, 1968).

10. The software program used was dBase II (Ashton-Tate, 1983). 11. The general assumption in all cases was that respondents meant, basically, what they said. Interpretation focused on how they said it. By this standard, less critical was sometimes more whether a respondent favored or opposed a policy of the administration than why the respondent took the view he or she did. For example, if a respondent had said only that the administration's policies appeared sound, inferences could not proceed very far. But if a member's support for the administration's policies was clearly attributed to agreement with the administration's methods in pursuing them, then reasonable inferences were possible.

12. See appendix B for the full list of questions.

13. Barney Frank, comments in the House of Representatives, 27 July 1983 (courtesy of Congressman Frank's office).

14. Lawrence J. Smith, comments in the House of Representatives, 27 July 1983 (courtesy of Congressman Frank's office).

15. Bill Nelson, "Central America: What Next?" 29 July 1983 (courtesy of Congressman Nelson's office).

16. Richard Cheney, "Congressman Dick Cheney Reports to Wyoming," November 1983 (courtesy of Congressman Cheney's office).

17. Gerry E. Studds, "Weekly Report to the People," 24 February 1984; "Kissinger Defends $9 Billion Aid Plan" (courtesy of Congressman Studds's office).

18. House, Committee on Foreign Affairs, *Central America, 1981: Report to the Committee on Foreign Affairs*, prepared by Hon Gerry E. Studds, 97th Cong., 1st sess., 1981, Committee Print, 31.

19. Sam B. Hall, Jr., comments in the House of Representatives on Central America, n.d. (courtesy of Congressman Hall's office).

20. Richard Ray to Mrozek, letter, 14 March 1984.

21. Thomas Eagleton to Mrozek, letter, 24 April 1984.
22. Henry Waxman to Mrozek, letter, 27 April 1984.
23. Charles E. Bennett, comments in the House of Representatives, 28 September 1983 (courtesy of Congressman Bennett's office).
24. Congressman Ike Skelton, "Key Lessons of the United States Involvement in Lebanon" (early 1984) (courtesy of Congressman Skelton's office).
25. Ibid.
26. John McCain, speaking on US forces for use in Lebanon, in House, *Congressional Record* 129, no. 127, 98th Cong., 1st sess., 28 September 1983 (courtesy of Congressman McCain's office).
27. David Durenberger, memorandum on Lebanon, 30 January 1984 (courtesy of Senator Durenberger's office).
28. David Durenberger, speaking on El Salvador and US policy in Central America, in Senate, *Congressional Record* 129, no. 103, 98th Cong., 1st sess., 20 July 1983 (courtesy of Senator Durenberger's office).
29. Ibid.
30. Ibid.
31. The general emphasis on the indivisibility of means and ends provides a sense of the abstract mechanism for determining criteria for appropriate action, but determining the specific substance of what is appropriate depends on concrete rather than abstract questions. These latter specific matters help to reveal inclinations toward one or the other of the two understandings of "normalcy" and to explain alignments in voting.
32. Don Bonker, "Let's Adhere to Our Declaration," statement in the House of Representatives, 28 July 1983 (courtesy of Congressman Bonker's office).
33. George J. Mitchell, speaking on US policy toward Central America, in Senate, *Congressional Record* 130, no. 44, 98th Cong., 2d sess., 5 April 1984 (courtesy of Senator Mitchell's office).
34. Richard Cheney, "Why We Can't Ignore Central America," in constituent newsletter for November 1983 (courtesy of Congressman Cheney's office).
35. Richard Cheney, "Congressman Dick Cheney Reports . . . ," November 1983 (courtesy of Congressman Cheney's office).
36. Bill Nelson, "Central America—What Next?" (courtesy of Congressman Nelson's office).
37. Richard H. Lehman, letter to constituents concerning Kissinger Commission Report, 29 February 1984 (courtesy of Congressman Lehman's office).
38. Jim Slattery to Mrozek, letter, 6 March 1984.
39. Ibid.
40. Alan Cranston, speaking on US military aid to El Salvador, in Senate, *Congressional Record* 129, no. 23, 98th Cong., 1st sess., 1 March 1983 (courtesy of Senator Cranston's office).
41. Alan Cranston, speaking on US policy toward Lebanon, in Senate, *Congressional Record* 129, no. 127, 98th Cong., 1st sess., 28 September 1983 (courtesy of Senator Cranston's office).
42. Richard Shelby, "A Message on Central America," n.d. (courtesy of Congressman Shelby's office).
43. William L. "Bill" Dickinson, weekly column, 1 March 1982 (courtesy of Congressman Dickinson's office).
44. Thomas K. Kindness, newsletter, August-September 1983 (courtesy of Congressman Kindness's office).
45. Pete Wilson, letter to US senators reporting on Central American fact-finding tour, 20 September 1983 (courtesy of Senator Wilson's office).
46. Congressman Thomas F. Hartnett, letter concerning Central America, 12 September 1983 (courtesy of Congressman Hartnett's office).
47. Jim Courter, "America As a Citizen of the World," commencement address at the Admiral Farragut Academy, Toms River, New Jersey, 4 June 1983.

48. James V. Hansen, constituent letter on El Salvador, April 1983 (courtesy of Congressman Hansen's office).

49. Robert J. Lagomarsino, Foreign Affairs Report, "US Policy in Central America," summer 1983 circular (courtesy of Congressman Lagomarsino's office).

50. Robin Britt to Mrozek, letter, 15 March 1984.

51. Richard Shelby to Mrozek, letter, enclosure, 7 March 1984.

52. Dan Schaefer to Mrozek, letter, 14 March 1984.

53. Transcript of radio broadcast by Congressman Sam B. Hall, Jr., n.d. (courtesy of Congressman Hall's office).

54. Larry E. Craig, response to constituent mail, 12 February 1984 (courtesy of Congressman Craig's office).

55. Larry E. Craig, response to constituent mail, 6 March 1983 (courtesy of Congressman Craig's office).

56. Jeremiah Denton, remarks in the Senate, 8 March 1984, *Congressional Record* 130, no. 27 (courtesy of Senator Denton's office).

57. Ibid.

58. Henry B. Gonzalez, "Pay Attention to Central America," 11 March 1984, column prepared for the *San Antonio Light* (courtesy of Congressman Gonzalez's office).

59. Gerry E. Studds, "Weekly Report to the People," 24 February 1984 (courtesy of Congressman Studds's office).

60. Gerry E. Studds, Bob Edgar, Ted Weiss, Richard L. Ottinger, and James L. Oberstar to colleagues in the House of Representatives, 25 January 1984 (courtesy of Congressman Studds's office).

61. Joseph R. Biden, Jr., speaking on US policy toward El Salvador, in Senate, *Congressional Record* 130, no. 43, 98th Cong., 2d sess. 4 April 1984 (courtesy of Senator Biden's office).

62. Ibid.

63. Daniel K. Inouye, "The Conflict in Central America," 1983 (courtesy of Senator Inouye's office).

64. Daniel K. Inouye, "News from Senator Daniel K. Inouye," 14 March 1983 (courtesy of Senator Inouye's office).

65. Leon Panetta to Mrozek, letter, 19 March 1984.

66. Ibid.

67. Gary Hart to Mrozek, letter, 12 March 1984.

CHAPTER 6

ALTERNATIVE VISIONS: THE WORLD BEYOND VIETNAM

The considerable residual interest in America's experience in Vietnam has existed alongside a vigorous resurgence of older concerns and a riveting curiosity about new trouble spots. By the early 1980s, Vietnam clearly exercised no monopoly in supplying analogies through which to defend current or proposed national policies on overseas matters. Other states (e.g., the Soviet Union, Great Britain, and Israel) provided enough grist for the mills of both military and political analysts. By the end of 1983, moreover, the United States had sufficiently engaged itself in other areas—Lebanon and Grenada, for example—so that Vietnam, while hardly "ancient history," was fast becoming yesterday's news.

Although a full picture of American attentions during the 1970s and after would require substantially more detailed study than has yet been done, preliminary observations show a wide range of interest in foreign affairs and a considerable assortment of metaphors for their treatment. Even as a source of frustration, for example, the war in Southeast Asia had serious competition from the Iranian hostage crisis suffered during the latter half of the Carter administration.[1] And the sense that the United States had substantial responsibility in the evolution of the Vietnam War was moderated by the Chinese military action against Vietnam. Similarly, the Soviet entry into Afghanistan provided interest in a different part of the world.

Other Wars, Other Analogies

The diverse experiences and events involving the United States and other countries after the mid-1970s provided a broad base from which lessons could be sought, from which explanatory analogies might be drawn, and from which future policy concerns might be derived. There was truly no limit on what could be construed as relevant, given the continued global scope of US interests, and the countries with national power less than that of the major world powers acted with sufficient independence to afford analogies of their own.

A variety of real or perceived lessons was posed by various parties as sources of guidance for US policy in Central America. References to such events as the Bay of Pigs invasion, undertaken by anti-Castro elements supported by the United States, frequently appeared in comments made in the Senate and the House or in materials sent to constituents. Senator Jeff Bingaman of New Mexico, for example, warned that a failure of the anti-Sandinista contras in Nicaragua, if they were backed by the United States, could confront the United States "with a repeat of the unfortunate Bay of Pigs scenario." He added: "One Nicaraguan, when asked where the Contras would go if they failed, replied 'Miami.'"[2]

In a similar vein, Senator John Danforth of Missouri saw a range of available historical illustrations that suggested what might happen if the US government withdrew from its Central American commitments. Senator Danforth, who supported efforts to strengthen the government of El Salvador militarily as well as economically, added that the experience of the Cambodians, Poles, Afghans, and others showed what could happen if such aid were not provided. As to supporting anti-Sandinista forces, Danforth allowed that US policy should not entail support for insurgents in an internal power struggle under normal circumstances. But he accepted it as necessary in the circumstances that actually existed.[3]

The Soviet presence in Afghanistan provided a focus of attention that superseded US involvement in Vietnam and clarified what many observers were coming to see as one of Vietnam's central lessons: vacillation and uncertainty in the prosecution of the war. In an article for the *New York Times* on 26 December 1983, military writer Drew Middleton asserted: "The most significant conclusion that can be drawn . . . is that, whatever else it is, Afghanistan is not the Russians' Vietnam."[4] First, the Soviets had evidently identified what they regarded as a genuine critical interest at stake—the prospect of an "anti-communist, Islamic country on the borders of the Soviet Union's Moslem republics in Soviet Central Asia. . . ."[5] Second, the Soviets' control of information at home reduced chances of "political turbulence." Synthesizing the assessment, Middleton quoted an unnamed expert: "We got tired of Vietnam. The Russians are not going to get tired of Afghanistan. It's too close to them and too close to the Indian Ocean. They'll stay."[6] One of the lessons of Afghanistan, then, appeared to be that action should be decisive and steady once a determination is made that significant national interests are at risk.

A difference occasionally cited between US and Soviet ways of handling guerrilla resistance was the Soviet use of a far greater, even ruthless, steadiness in what George Will called a "savage strategy."[7] Citing the wide scattering of antipersonnel mines throughout Afghanistan, Will noted: "These weapons of indiscriminate yet limited violence express a strategy of unlimited war by the world's largest army against an entire population."[8] He assessed the reasoning through which the Soviets had evidently come to their approach. They answered Mao's dictum that the guerrilla was like a fish swimming in the sea of the people not by "winning the allegiance of the water," as the French and the Americans had attempted in Southeast Asia, but by "[killing] the fish by draining the water."[9] Will asserted that the "Soviet Union has analyzed various failures, including America's, in counterguerrilla warfare and has concluded that the key to success is a kind of ruthlessness that only a totalitarian regime will practice."[10] If Vietnam lingered here, it was as a lesson for the Soviets and not as a specter haunting US thinking in world affairs.

In place of any real or imagined unitary model for guiding US policy, reports circulated that government policymakers and analysts were increasingly prone to call on a host of past American experiences. In October 1983, for example, one detailed commentary listed several analogies that had supposedly disposed US officials to favor sending US armed forces into Grenada. Allegedly, President Ronald Reagan was concerned that Grenada not become "another Iran," where Americans might be held hostage by a harsh and unpredictable regime. In the desire to cut off chances that the island would become an outpost of Cuba and the Soviet Union and to lessen a tide toward radicalism, Secretary of State George Shultz and others supposedly sought to avert "another Nicaragua." Others, fearful of a drift into leftist extremism after the coup d'état staged against the government of Maurice Bishop in Grenada, were said to worry over "another Suriname." Yet another analogy discussed in Washington soon after the start of US operations in Grenada was President Lyndon Johnson's decision to send 21,000 troops to the Dominican Republic in 1965 in order to prevent a move to the left in that country's government, which Johnson apparently believed would deteriorate into civil chaos.[11]

To be sure, the precise meaning and validity of reports in the open press concerning views of governmental officials are themselves matters of estimation—perhaps even some plain guesswork. Nonetheless, it is suggestive of the framework of concerns in the early 1980s that the analogies cited during discussion of Grenada did not primarily establish legality as the essential basis for action. Instead, circumstances of need were more important, and the final demonstration of the wisdom of an action was that it did manage to stave off the undesired political or social outcome against which the action was undertaken. Seen critically, such an approach might be a challenge to the US moral advantage in world affairs. Seen more sympathetically, however, it suggested a special sort of pragmatism. It also surely marked a passage beyond the dominance of any one historical example as the guiding force for present policy.

One commentator who did make explicit use of lessons drawn from the Vietnam War applauded the Reagan administration's move on Grenada. In "Central America and the Lessons of Vietnam," published in the Autumn-Winter 1983 issue of *Survey*, Sol Sanders, formerly a correspondent in Southeast Asia and then an editor of *Business Week*, liked the "more decisive attitude" the action represented, calling it a "forthright attempt to deal with a potentially major problem for the region and for American security." The greatest worry Sanders seemed to have was that the United States might ultimately be proved an "unreliable partner," and he backed a long-term commitment to meet what he saw as a protracted Communist threat.[12] As often as not, analogies other than those of Vietnam lent themselves to deliberations on US policy; and even when they did not, the analogies of Vietnam, themselves numerous and diverse, did little to tie the hands of those affected by them. The urgency that various observers attached to the problems was as likely as anything to govern what the analogies supposedly meant.

Beyond Crisis

The reluctance on the part of some Americans to identify various problems facing the United States as "crises" increased the chances of disagreement over what constituted appropriate action when those problems invited a US response; and the difficulties would be at their worst and sharpest if there were occasion to question the goodwill of those most responsible for making and enforcing policy. In his column for 17 February 1984, conservative political commentator William Safire seriously questioned not the substance of then current US policies, including those in the Middle East, but the character of the arguments advanced in their support.[13] Safire compared Soviet definitions of Yuri Andropov's fatal illness as "croup" to the US government's decision to withdraw its Marines from Lebanon and it referred to Congressman Thomas P. O'Neill's call for withdrawal as a "surrender." The comparison was less than flattering. Safire also saw a major difference between Secretary of the Navy John Lehman's explanation that shelling targets in Lebanon from ships stationed offshore would provide "supporting fire to the Lebanese forces" and President Reagan's assertion, at nearly the same time, that the shelling was to enhance the safety of American and other MNF personnel in Lebanon.[14] Safire wanted more than a coherent "straight line"; he wanted one that was simple, straightforward, and truthful. He warned sharply that "mendacity is not the road to credibility" and cautioned against "twisting the truth to create the appearance of legality."[15] He suggested that the problem originated largely in the sense of crisis, but insisted that "'the truth will make you free' is not an empty piety."[16] Apart from the tart force of his remarks, it is perhaps most useful to note that Safire did not dispute specific elements of the US policies being advanced—he challenged the methods used to defend those policies, and he worried that shaping governmental words and actions according to the turns of crisis "damages our system" more than actions undertaken hurt the enemy.[17] The preservation of "our system" would be the key to coherent policy and action over the long run.[18]

Criticism was occasionally voiced over the quality and thrust of information released concerning US involvements in various overseas trouble spots, and there appeared to be many reasons for it. To be sure, personal pique and institutional self-interest on the part of the press and electronic media may have played a part, but this was hardly the whole story; nor would it have been sufficient to explain any measure of popular sympathy that eventually developed for their position. Nor would it explain away the issue of relative responsibility of Congress and the president in the development of either a national consensus or a national overseas policy. For example, congressional leaders who had overseen the House subcommittee's investigation of the bombing of the US Marine barracks in Beirut in October concluded that "erroneous, misleading, and often contradictory" information had been given by Marine commanders in Beirut and Washington.[19] Evidently, part of the difficulty had stemmed from the particular way in which the initial information had been given during the first days after the attack and by the impression of certitude projected by such a high-ranking spokesman as Marine Corps Commandant Gen Paul X. Kelley. In a statement on 1 November 1983, General Kelley cautiously asked for patience "while I try to tell a story of what we think, at this time, happened"; in his opening remarks in Senate testimony the previous day, however, he began without such qualification, saying, "I would now like to describe what occurred on Sunday morning, October 23. . . ."[20] It was open to speculation whether General Kelley's more confident remarks reflected a wish to seem "in control" in time of crisis. Some nurtured suspicion of a cover-up, less because a discrepancy had developed than because of the firmness with which the contradictory explanations had been expressed. It was a classic "no-win situation." Assuming there was no wish to deceive, the question of competence lingered; and close scrutiny of an event entailing the death of hundreds of US servicemen was inevitable.[21] Was there any imaginable gain in presenting anything other than the fullest truth—which meant noting the unknowns and admitting to one's own uncertainties?

The accumulating testimony offered by US servicemen stationed in Lebanon did little to support the "take-charge" attitude depicted by various officials—remarks which suggested that their confusion and imprecision as to the whole point of a US Marine presence in Lebanon was appreciable. But the impression created by comments from the Marines also suggested the extreme difficulty of meshing a crisis consciousness with a passive or defensive disposition of forces. Contrasting the peacekeeping operation in Lebanon and the Marine role in the US action in Grenada shortly after the bombing of the Marine barracks in Beirut, Marine Cpl John Hargrove said that Grenada was a "real go-at-it kind of job" but the mission in Lebanon was "just a sit-back situation. I never met a Lebanese."[22] LCpl Samuel Lee remarked:

> In Grenada, we could go right to the source of the problem. We could go into people's homes, we could go out on search-and-destroy missions, and we could use all our weapons. The enemy was real clear. But we couldn't do those things here. We just didn't know who was the enemy. The Moslems? The Christians? The Lebanese Army?[23]

The discomfort with what they saw as a passive role may well have contributed to the Marines' perception that the mission itself was unclear. Lt John LaTorre noted that in Lebanon, unlike Grenada, Marines and other service personnel were called on to perform in ways for which they had not been effectively trained. "This antiterrorism work we had to do here was kind of new to us," he added. "We were writing the book on it as we went along."[24] Evidently lacking either the sense that they were prepared or the conviction that past experiences such as those in Vietnam might provide the suitable guide for their performance, such remarks invited the question, "Was the insufficient preparation for such contingencies as were encountered in Lebanon more the source of urgency and the sense of crisis than were the actual US interests at stake there?" Sgt James Utley, who had been in the first deployment of Marines in Lebanon during late August and early September 1982 to aid in the evacuation of Palestinian Liberation Organization fighters, returned later in September and came back for a third time in November 1983. "It got a lot different when I came back in November." Asked what the Marines were expected to do at the airport where they were stationed during the second phase of commitment, he said "It's hard to pin down." And LCpl Donald Melton said of their mission: "Whatever it was, I guess we accomplished it. I thought we were here to keep the airport open. We didn't do that. Nothing we can do now except just get outta here."[25] Perhaps the range in understanding among the ranks was exemplified by the sharply differing comments of two Marine corporals. Cpl Fred Garrison commented: "Our job was to keep the perimeter secure. Anything else we did just came along in time"; but Cpl Gerivele Brown said: "We were supposed to show American interests. It was a political thing for sure."[26] When clarity faltered and the sense of purpose became confused, the temptation rose to locate crises very close to home—not with the achievement of an abstract objective, but in the safety of oneself and one's unit. That matters were critical for those deployed in an area fraught with dangers needed no elaboration; that it was critical to US interests to have them deployed there was the proposition that had not won a consensus of support.

Urgency and crisis had been a basis for rallying Americans to march in common with little discussion and less dissent; but after the skeptical side of the American tradition made its return, crisis itself became a candidate for scrutiny. How much of a crisis was it? For whom was it a crisis? What were the stakes? The details that create practical meaning would determine whether suspending some aspect of traditionally American ways of doing things might be allowed. Whether individual and group interests were to be subordinated to a common good depended essentially on whether common good could be demonstrated. Even if such temporary adjustments occurred, however, there could be a serious toll to pay if the originally credible demonstration was eventually shot through with holes.

There were risks that this could occur in a great many situations, but the realm of press censorship with respect to US operations in Grenada in late 1983 proved to be a vivid illustration. Although the restriction of press access to Grenada at the time of US military operations there late in 1983 won much positive reaction initially, concern later arose that the full story of what had occurred there might not have been released. The early disclosures of arms stocks and of documents suggesting the basis for long-term links between Grenada and the Communist-bloc countries did much to support the US government's stand that legitimate security interests had been involved in these regional affairs—in short, that the regional problem was part of a larger set of global issues. But would the entire explanation hold?

The substance of what occurred in the management of news concerning the Grenada operation deserves full-scale treatment in its own right, but it is particularly pertinent here to emphasize that the goal of keeping the public understanding of the operation as simple as possible was itself widely taken as an intended remedy for the ills of Vietnam and for the confusion that press reports about Vietnam were said to have generated. Historian George C. Herring, writing in the *Baltimore Sun* on 3 November 1983, saw improper readings of Vietnam's lessons as a partial explanation for the zealous defense offered of censorship exercised during the US military operations on Grenada. Herring disputed allegations that the manner in which the American media reported the Vietnam War had turned the American public against it, suggesting that the growing cost of the war in lives lost and taxes paid was the truly decisive factor—"not media portrayal of the war but the war itself that produced growing skepticism among the American public."[27] Not denying that there was some opposition to the war from the start, Herring notes that "most major newspapers supported the war editorially until late 1967, some well beyond. Content analysis indicates that at least until 1968 network news broadcasts tended overwhelmingly to be neutral or to support the war."[28] The central thrust of his remarks was not to deny that the media played a role, nor to ignore the issue of bias, but rather to insist that the first sources of trouble for the Vietnam War were how it was conceived and how it was fought. Consequently, Herring rejected the implication that military success depended on conducting operations under secrecy and in the absence of reporters and observers. "When we fail," Herring noted, "we naturally look inward for explanations...." Unwilling to find such an explanation in ourselves, we seek it in "scapegoats."[29] This was a proclivity that the failures in Vietnam had apparently been unable to dislodge, and it reappeared—an American lesson drawn from British behavior in the Falklands, itself rooted in a perception of what had happened in Southeast Asia.

Similarly, Henry Grunwald attributed the Reagan administration's endorsement of censorship in the Grenada operation to its perception of what happened in America over Vietnam. "Obviously," Grunwald wrote in *Time* on 7 November 1983, "the White House or the Pentagon remembered the Viet Nam 'living-room war'" and "admired and envied Margaret Thatcher's dealing with the press during the Falklands invasion...." But Grunwald suggested that the decision to restrict the press during the Grenada action was counterproductive. "Whenever the press is excluded," Grunwald observed, "speculation and rumor take over." Before long, as US military spokesmen acknowledged that resistance was continuing several days after troops were committed, "the result was vague and nagging alarm, a suspicion that the world's largest military power had trouble subduing a flyspeck island."[30] Perhaps a more usefully drawn lesson from the Vietnam experience might have focused on the way in which transmission of information to media representatives can produce results contrary to the hopes and expectations of military spokesmen—and on how the manner in which military officers handle information intended for the media can sometimes jeopardize their own credibility.

Somewhat ironically, despite concerns that the press and electronic media might be unfair to the US military when reporting on US operations, some observers believed that the press could become an extremely effective ally—and even believed that Army officers were beginning to see the press less as a problem or barrier and more as an opportunity. In one commentary on the matter, for example, Army Col Harry Summers spoke of the "growing awareness that the very news media that many in the Army complained about so bitterly during the Vietnam War for their vivid portrayals of the realities of the battlefield is precisely the instrument that can 'make the price of involvement clear.'" To its own surprise, Summers continued, "the Army is becoming aware that television portrayals of battlefield realities is an asset, not a liability."[31] The role of the press, in this construction, included establishing a clear baseline of popular support—not to serve as a cheering section or propaganda vehicle but as a catalyst for shaping whatever the real wishes and interests of the people were. In this process, the press could thus contribute mightily to the development of clarity and coherence in policy. Admittedly, this was something of an ideal statement of what was thinkable; whether it could be carried off was far more a matter of controversy.

What Summers's remarks suggested was that Army officers—perhaps some in other services as well—had come to think of potential military involvements in specific, case-by-case terms. Whether this meshed with the underlying instincts of the press was not the only question, however; whether it paralleled the thrust among policymakers deserved at least as much attention. Danger might arise if the case-by-case approach suggested among some military officers, and reflected in Summers's rather optimistic notions of dealing with the press, ran headlong against a "blanket" approach at the policy level. For example, Tom Wicker wrote of his fears that US policy objectives were stated in such categorical and overly general terms that, sooner or later, major problems must arise. In the *New York Times* of 15 March 1983, writing about what he called two "dangerous doctrines," Wicker focused on President Reagan's identifying El Salvador as essential to US national security and the possibility that the United States might be unable to strengthen Salvadoran government forces sufficiently to end the guerrilla resistance. How, under such circumstances, could the President "stand by and see El Salvador become the first domino in a string reaching to the Rio Grande? Or, will he not then be forced by his own words to stronger action?"[32] Wicker did not dispute that interventions with a military component could be justified; but he was troubled by what he saw as the implications of very broad statements on policy, seeing the greatest source of danger in the attitude from which the policy stemmed more than in the specific actions that had actually been taken. Wicker suggested that the administration was casting its Central American policies and actions into the framework of a bipolar confrontation between the United States and the Soviet Union and, by doing so, was "inviting exactly a repetition of the Vietnam experience" by making the real criterion for United States involvement Washington's stance toward Moscow rather than its appraisal of El Salvador.[33]

The assertion that the American press had a right to be present during a US military enterprise on foreign soil entailed both an interpretation of what had been traditional procedure on such matters in previous American wars and on what constituted appropriate "normalcy." The defense of a departure from such procedures as were sanctioned in American tradition could be made credible by appealing to the novelty of special circumstances in the contemporary world, by claiming that US forces would be unusually threatened by the presence of press members, by seeing some special urgency in the moment and invoking an aura of crisis, or by some combination. In all cases, however, the keynote was a departure from some elements of "normalcy" and tradition. It was precisely this sense of special urgency and crisis that appeared to face challenge and to raise doubts and worries among various observers outside the administration.

Beyond Deterrence

The interaction of "crisis" and "normalcy" lay beneath broad defense concepts as well as specific incidents. Deterrence theory, that special child of the nuclear age, has depended on belief in a network of assessments and assumptions that had special force after World War II. Advocates of defending the country by dissuading a potential enemy from attacking needed to believe that they had sufficient force with which to make their threat of retaliatory response credible, and the enemy needed to believe it, too.[34] Proponents of deterrence had to justify such a theory by acknowledging their own vulnerability to a strike—a strike that atomic weapons would make exceptionally devastating even if the enemy had lost an immense percentage of his attacking force.[35] In the end, though, there were two categories of concerns without whose survival the whole special theory of deterrence would inevitably fall into doubt. These had to do with matters of disposition and philosophical outlook, the technical details of the apparatus of deterrence, and the measure of complexity invoked to use and protect the apparatus itself.

The general notion that a potential enemy could be discouraged from carrying out hostile actions by raising a credible threat of a strong reaction in kind is deeply ingrained in the history of human expectations. Although the case for peaceful resolution of difference has been couched principally on grounds of logic and in assertions of reasonableness, the case of deterrence of enemy attack uses logic and an underlying appeal to a less benign interpretation of "human nature." The two approaches are obviously related; but there is a critical difference between the two in the balance of hope and expectation.[36] Although it is perhaps more common for advocates of peaceful resolution of conflict through diplomacy and similar processes to be charged with having a "blanket" view of mankind as good, it is more important for purposes here that deterrence tends toward a "blanket" suspicion of human motivation. The extensiveness of the view is as significant as the attitude it represents, since it makes the more suspicious inclinations more impervious to contradiction by specific cases that seem not to fit the pattern. Since motivation itself is suspect, even an action that seems practically beneficial can be seen as a source of anxiety. None of this was novel to the post-World War II era when taken in its generalities, but it did take on special sharpness and urgency because of the special immensity and visibility of nuclear weapons.[37]

As a theory and as an articulated element in strategy, then, deterrence was an assertion of consciousness rather than a fact. By literal definition, a fact was something that had occurred; by implication, it could be demonstrated empirically. With deterrence, however, it was impossible to prove that the absence of war was caused by one's defensive preparations rather than a prior or separate unwillingness of one's opponent to attack. Peace could be "a fact," but it could hardly be more than theory that deterrence should take the credit for it. Even though the theoretical statements on deterrence focused on its credibility to the potential enemy, then, it was the United States that needed to be persuaded. In this sense, deterrence could only have emerged as part of a conscious effort to make sense out of unusual security needs in an unusually dangerous world in hopes of winning some peculiar peace of mind.[38]

In all, the rise of consciously articulated deterrence theory and policy depended on a special, atypical combination of views that gave a particular interpretation to world conditions. Coming after a war described as one between forces of good and those of evil, deterrence was facilitated by the deeply negative appraisals of the Soviet Union and of the Communists in China. It was boosted by the domestic fear of subversion as much as by the Soviet attainment of atomic and then thermonuclear weapons, especially because disclosure of Soviet espionage operations in the United States and Canada helped to link the two.[39] So, then, the clarity of deterrence was related to the simplicity of the public, and possibly the official, perception of the world at the time. The persuasiveness and adequacy of the theory was thus rooted in a very special time and an unusual set of circumstances. Although the underlying truth remained that the possession of force may dissuade a potential attacker from carrying out an aggressive act, the specific validity of deterrence in its highly articulated versions might not survive a change in those unusual circumstances without a change in the manner and character of argument used in support of it. For if some were predisposed to doubt an argument rooted in a "blanket" suspicion of human nature, was not doubt likely to sharpen if specific events and practical contacts between the opposing parties tore holes in the argument?

Such a development was all the more likely as greater numbers of Americans focused on case-specific analysis and as the broader cold war consensus came under challenge. Although the Vietnam experience may have hastened the reexamination of that consensus, it was not Vietnam itself that thus posed a challenge to the theory and policy of deterrence but rather the far broader return to patterns of thought that had been common before the world wars. The problem in the 1980s was how to maintain the substance of deterrence while the generalized rhetoric used in its defense appeared to be facing challenge and losing effectiveness.

The specific illustrations of this dilemma surrounded the discussions of strategic weapon systems, particularly as to which new systems should be developed and later deployed. Perhaps the most controversial and the most emblematic debate came over the proposals for an "MX" missile, later designated as "Peacekeeper" by President Ronald Reagan. No discussion of MX/Peacekeeper would be complete—or balanced—without recognizing certain deep-seated differences between its proponents and opponents. Beyond all the technical details of the missile and its warheads, the rock-bottom question was whether building not only this missile but *any* new missile would add to US national security and to the *sense* of security on the part of various American constituencies. Proponents of such a missile tended to see greater security in the qualitative improvement of US strategic arms, sometimes speaking of a "window of vulnerability" which the United States had incautiously opened for a possible attacker; the missile's opponents saw greater insecurity as stemming from the very building of the weapon itself.[40] This most basic underlying difference of views, for all its importance, was only one of several forces affecting the debate and illustrating some aspects of the broader readjustment in approaches toward defense and other public policy issues.

The nature of the debate and the lines of argument used reflect the critical importance of the reemergence of "particularism" or case-by-case assessment of US interests and commitments. Seen in its very broadest and most general aspect, the MX/Peacekeeper was meant to strengthen one element in the US strategic Triad, which various governmental officials, as well as some civilian analysts, had concluded was in jeopardy. For some, including certain highly placed officials, the clear imperative of preserving the strategic Triad outweighed numerous other considerations; and the adoption of this view was by no means a rigidly partisan view. For although the missile came to be associated with the Republican administration of Ronald Reagan as it moved into production and deployment in the 1980s, it was the administration of Democrat Jimmy Carter that settled on both the missile and a highly visible and controversial plan for its deployment.[41] This issue was not party affiliation but an essentially unquestioning bedrock commitment to the concept of the strategic Triad as the heart of deterrence.

Against this broad view, opponents of the MX/Peacekeeper raised what some considered "nit-picking" criticisms. Assuming that the weapon could be built and deployed, what benefit would come from Carter's deployment scheme and how long would it last? If the goal was to have an invulnerable strategic reserve, what deployment scheme would promise this? What were the various data bases on which the assessments of potential invulnerability to incoming nuclear attacks had been made? What suppositions had been made as to the dynamics of behavior on the part of a potential enemy, including possible responses to measures the United States might take? Even accepting that such critical questions were intended to lower the likelihood that congressional authorization and funding of MX/Peacekeeper would be approved, the choice of strategies by which to attack the MX/Peacekeeper program was itself informative. It was neither "security" nor "defense" that was criticized, but rather the unspoken call for faith in professional technological expertise and, even more, in the judgment of the highest military professional and civilian governmental authorities. Against this, the more skeptical parties called not for "revival" but for a specification by "chapter and verse" proving that the MX preacher was truly alive with the "spirit."[42]

The argument about the MX/Peacekeeper thus entailed an extraordinary amount of attention to the practical aspects of its design characteristics and its deployment options. Whether such close concern over how the MX would operate and how the basing would be done was proper or merely intrusive was a matter of opinion. From one perspective, the grasp by outsiders and nonexperts at the very innards of a strategic policy seemed stunningly inappropriate. From another perspective, however, the running disagreements among defense analysts brought their expertise into some doubt. Meanwhile, as changes occurred in the official version of how MX would be deployed, military officers seemed to experience overnight conversion to a new deployment creed; and they suffered their own loss of credibility for their apparent apostasy. With a swiftness that literally defied belief, military personnel darted from one deployment scheme to another—such as the system of multiple protective shelters, that of densely locating the missiles in hardened silos, and so forth—seeking to stay in line with current official wisdom and yet to keep an eye toward possibly better options. Notions of burying the missiles deeply underground,[43] setting them out in shallow coastal waters, or carrying them aboard aircraft also appeared.

But perhaps the greatest question emerged less from the diversity of voices on the subject than from precisely how they diverged in what they said and what they thought. Looking at only two schemes (multiple protective shelters and closely spaced basing), the official defense community appeared not only to have changed its mind but to have radically altered its logic. The fundamental premise of the multiple shelter system was essentially the same as that of a shell game (keep the potential enemy guessing while the stakes were high enough that action without certainty was far beyond the tolerances of good sense). Scattered over an area described as roughly the equivalent of Pennsylvania, the system used dispersal coupled with deception. The supposition that closely spacing the MXs would induce "fratricide," in which early detonations of enemy warheads would destroy or disable the balance of incoming rounds, turned the logic of the vast multiple shelter scheme upside down. What if warheads were brought in piecemeal over a long period of time? Would this "pin down" the US missiles? What if the enemy sent in warheads that would be activated by the launching of MXs? And what credibility did the argument that Soviet countermeasures to it were not feasible have, given the state of Soviet technology—especially when the argument in favor of MX as a whole was linked to the belief that Soviet technological versatility (specifically, the ability to develop MIRVs) had been grossly underestimated by earlier analysts? Matters seemed to be approaching what turn-of-the-century military thinker Homer Lea called "intangible complexity which heralded the splintering of consensus." But by the 1980s, perhaps it had already been splintered.[44]

Clarity of purpose, coherent strategy, and steadiness of effort are virtues in peace no less than in war. But on the matter of MX—and most visibly on the question of basing—civilian and military defense personnel spoke in a multitude of voices. (Experts favoring a new missile debated what kind of basing mode was needed to guarantee the system against attack. But in making their cases, they used clearly contradictory arguments—and an argument rooted in expert authority can easily be refuted when the expert's testimony is inconsistent.)

Some officials have indicated a wish that the debate had never gone into technical matters. They evidently meant "technical" to include both the mechanics of the missile and the strategic logic for its integration into overall defense. Yet what appears to be the emerging reassertion of case-by-case examination of US interests and actions in world affairs seems to run headlong against reliance on expert judgment. The world of defense and "security beyond deterrence" may well prove to be inimical to "blanket" explanations of weapon systems and strategic thought on how to use them. As officials have broadened the scope and means of deterrence to include the full spectrum of conflict, the single focus of the era that gave it birth appears to have been replaced by a more kaleidoscopic vision. Deterrence may have acquired too many meanings to permit the cultivation of "prior trust" for the proposals and policies of any government agency or administration. Was it possible in a world of many lessons, many analogies, and many models to find a shared perspective on events? In a world of many competing interests, was it possible to achieve some consensus? And since moving away from a Vietnam-linked world also entailed moving away from cold war consciousness to something more multifaceted, were there any bases left for a common national grounding on defense-related matters?

Masters of Our Fate

In a test conducted at the State University of New York at Stony Brook in 1970, a team of researchers told two groups that they would be given relatively painful stimuli—but at different levels of intensity. Although the actual level of stimulus used with each group was the same, the group that believed it was receiving less of a pain-causing stimulus actually showed less physical reaction and sensed itself to be in less discomfort. The researchers concluded: "Perhaps the next best thing to being master of one's fate is being deluded into thinking that one is. . . ."[45] In some measure, the pursuit of real but intangible goals must always approximate such self-persuasion. The borderline that can't be crossed without risking calamity is the one suggested in "The Emperor's New Clothes": one may pursue a real intangible, but one may not pretend that the nonexistent is tangibly present. In other words, the interpretation of facts into intangible meanings may be legitimate; the delusion that hopes are facts is not. Such a logic might be applied as an experimental test of the difference between aspiration and desperation—between intention and illusion—in international relationships.

The perceived level of gain sustained in world affairs is partly a function of the anticipated level of gain; and that depends, partly, on what objectives are seen to constitute a gain. In the American case, the preservation of substantial influence in world affairs has been a fundamental component in the vision of gain that has largely prevailed since World War II.[46] The alternatives of "drift and mastery" have a long history within the American political mentality; and the image of a capable, forceful leadership couched in the rhetoric of "taking control" is commonplace. The ultimate challenge, however, was to make fact rather than fantasy the true measure of mastery.

The process of acting in world affairs has typically required understanding of interests either promised or put to risk by various policy alternatives. Even in times of patent danger, such as the period after the Japanese attack on Pearl Harbor, US officials saw the wisdom of sponsoring a media campaign to outline "why we fight." A rudimentary response could have been that the United States fought because it had been attacked, but governmental officials recognized that the public had a need to understand what could have been lost if the United States had failed to react. In the years after World War II, the residual sense of "why we fought" and why a cold war against a hostile ideology had to be accepted, however reluctantly, lingered; yet the more tangled and the more subtle the reasonings, the harder it became for anyone but the most sophisticated to see the fine thread that tied them together. And so, although the Vietnam War has at times been credited with destroying the cold war consensus, it is at least as possible that the old consensus, which was already showing strains after the Cuban missile crisis and in the days of peaceful coexistence, could have been killed by peace without any additional help. If the consensus faltered because public consciousness was less swayed by assertions of crisis, what new consensus could be established? The answers pointed in the direction of interests (positive manifestations of what the United States might want) rather than crisis.

Notes

1. So powerful was the image of US citizens—especially officials—held captive in Iran that fear of "another Iran" was used as a partial explanation for President Ronald Reagan's decision

to send troops into Grenada in 1983. See Bernard Gwertzman "Fear of 'Another Iran' Haunted White House," *New York Times*, 26 October 1983, 1, 5.

2. Jeff Bingaman, comments in the Senate, 31 October 1983, *Congressional Record* 129, no. 149 (courtesy of Senator Bingaman's office).

3. John C. Danforth to Mrozek, letter, 26 March 1984.

4. Drew Middleton, "Four Years of Afghan Battle: No Vietnam for Moscow," *New York Times*, 26 December 1983, 8.

5. Ibid.

6. Ibid.

7. George F. Will, "Savage Strategy," *Washington Post*, 5 January 1984, 23.

8. Ibid.

9. Ibid.

10. Ibid.

11. Ibid. Will's argument raises a curious question as to what policies were worth undertaking for a country such as the United States. Since ruthlessness was evidently beyond its capacity and since the effort to "win hearts and minds" in Vietnam had not been adequate, one wonders if the United States had any options left for countering insurgency and guerrillas. On Soviet behavior in Afghanistan, also see Cord Meyer, "Recognizing the Courage of Afghan Freedom Fighters," *Washington Times*, 5 January 1984, 1-C.

12. Gwertzman, "Fear of 'Another Iran,'" 1.

13. William Safire, "Truth in Crises," *New York Times*, 17 February 1984, 27.

14. Ibid.

15. Ibid.

16. Ibid.

17. Ibid.

18. It is perhaps worth noting here that Safire's argument is not one based on "prissy" legal technicality. His point is that departing from the constitutional "rules of the game" badly damages the prospects for gaining either the support of major power centers, such as Congress, or the support of the American public. In these specifications, Safire's views strongly resembled those expressed by various military officers such as Gen Edward Meyer and Gen John Vessey, Jr.

19. Michael Getler, "First Accounts of Attack on Marines 'Misleading,'" *Washington Post*, 22 December 1983, 1.

20. Ibid.

21. The congressional subcommittees interviewed survivors of the incident, visited the site, had the benefit of various technical experts, and came to the conclusion that the firmly professed early descriptions were seriously flawed.

22. Bernard Gwertzman, "U.S. Is Considering Emergency Arms for El Salvador," *New York Times*, 22 February 1984, 1.

23. Ibid.

24. Ibid. Such remarks help to explain why some Marines believed that lessons about many kinds of irregular action, including aspects of antiterrorism, that had been hard won in Vietnam had been forgotten.

25. Ibid.

26. Ibid.

27. George C. Herring, "The First Casualty," *Baltimore Sun*, 3 November 1983.

28. Ibid.

29. Ibid.

30. Henry Grunwald, "Trying to Censor Reality," *Time*, 7 November 1983. The suspicion that the Grenada operation was actually a demonstration of American military weaknesses and ineptitude may thus be strengthened even more than might otherwise have been the case by such assessments as those made by the congressional military reform caucus. See, for

example, Rick Maze, "Report Faults Military Performance in Grenada," *Air Force Times*, 23 April 1984, which commented on a study prepared by William S. Lind of the Military Reform Institute and released through Congressman Jim Courter, head of the House Military Reform Caucus. On the tightening of controls on communications between governmental officials and the press, see Philip Taubman, "Pentagon Tightens Control on Aides' Central America Statements," *New York Times*, 25 February 1984, 5.

31. Col Harry G. Summers, Jr., "Continuity and Change: Clausewitz and Strategy Today," International Studies Associational Meeting, 22 October 1982 (Strategic Studies Institute, Carlisle Barracks, Pa.).

32. Tom Wicker, "Two Dangerous Doctrines," *New York Times*, 15 March 1983.

33. Ibid.

34. It was also possible to pursue deterrence even if an enemy was not overwhelmingly troubled by the forces and strategies one developed. Unlike actual warfare, the "stand off" in deterrence lacks external verifying behavior which, to be sure, is just as well for avoiding a nuclear war, yet contributes to an inability to nail down with methodological rigor how well deterrence is working, or even if it works at all.

35. If one compares a typical bombload of the World War II period (pre-Hiroshima) with even a Hiroshima-size bomb as the "typical" post-World War II bombload (admitting that quantities were small until much later), it becomes clear that even a single aircraft breaking through air defenses could do terrible damage—with one post-World War II aircraft loaded with atomic weapons being the "equivalent" of hundreds—even thousands—of World War II-era sorties. In such an environment, anything less than a 100 percent effective defense became less than satisfying.

36. There is considerable literature on American peace movements and on ideas about peaceful resolution of conflict. See, for example, Ernest C. Bolt, *Ballots before Bullets: The War Referendum Approach to Peace in America, 1914-1941* (Charlottesville: University Press of Virginia, 1977); Nicholas Murray Butler, *The Path to Peace: Essays and Addresses on Peace and Its Making* (New York: Charles Scribner's Sons, 1930); Senate Committee on Foreign Relations, *Planning for Peace*. Hearings, 89th Cong., lst sess., 11-12 May 1965; Sylvanus Milne Duvall, *War and Human Nature* (New York: Public Affairs Committee, Inc., 1947); Paul Einzig, *Appeasement before, during and after the War* (London: Macmillan and Co., Ltd., 1942); Federal Bureau of Investigation, *The Communist Concepts of War, Pacifism, and "Peace"* (Washington, D.C.: Federal Bureau of Investigation, 1949); Lionel Morris Gelber, *Reprieve from War, a Manual for Realists* (New York: Macmillan, 1950); Christina Grant, *The Anglo-American Peace Movement in the Mid-Nineteenth Century* (New York: Columbia University Press, 1930); Sondra R. Herman, *Eleven against War: Studies in American Internationalist Thought, 1898-1921* (Stanford, Calif.: Hoover Institution Press, 1969); Walter Armin Linn, *False Prophets of Peace* (Harrisburg, Pa.: The Military Service Publishing Company, 1939); John McAuley Palmer, *Statesmanship or War* (Garden City, N.Y.: Doubleday, Page and Co., 1927); Dexter Perkins, *America's Quest for Peace* (Bloomington: Indiana University Press, 1962); William E. Rappard, *The Quest for Peace since the World War* (Cambridge, Mass.: Harvard University Press, 1940); James P. Warburg, *Peace in Our Time?* (New York: Harper & Brothers, 1940); Lawrence S. Wittner, *Rebels against War, the American Peace Movement, 1941-1960* (New York: Columbia University Press, 1969).

A variety of works help to reveal the differences in hope and expectation harbored by those advocating different methods for achieving security and avoiding war, as well as varying notions of what contributes to the enhancement of security and the lessening of anxiety. See, for example, Ralph Morris Goldman, *Arms Control and Peacekeeping: Feeling Safe in This World* (New York: Random House, 1982); L. Gunnar Johnson, *Conflicting Concepts of Peace in Contemporary Peace Studies* (Beverly Hills, Calif.: Sage Publications, 1976); Mark Arthur May, *A Social Psychologyy of War and Peace* (New Haven, Conn.: Yale University Press [for the Institute of Human Relations], 1944); Tom Hatherley, *Psychological Factors of Peace and*

War (London: Hutchinson, 1950); Robert F. Randle, *The Origins of Peace: A Study of Peacemaking and the Structures of Peace Settlements* (New York: Free Press, 1973); Phillip Van Slyck, *Peace: The Control of National Power, a Guide for the Concerned Citizen on Problems of Disarmament and Strengthening the United Nations* (Boston: Beacon Press, 1963); Arthur I. Waskow, *The Worried Man's Guide to World Peace* (Garden City, N.Y.: Anchor Books, 1963); Quincy Wright, *The Causes of War and the Conditions of Peace* (London: Longmans, Green, 1935).

37. On defense policy and American attitudes at the end of the 1940s, see Richard F. Haynes, *The Awesome Power* (Baton Rouge: Louisiana State University Press, 1973); Walter La Feber, *America, Russia, and the Cold War, 1945-1966* (New York: John Wiley, 1967); Thomas M. Campbell, *Masquerade Peace* (Tallahassee: Florida State University Press, 1973); Donald J. Mrozek, "Peace through Strength," PhD dissertation, Rutgers University, 1972.

38. The point of the remarks here is not to say that deterrence does not work but to suggest the difficulty in making the case for it among those who are not already believers in its efficacy. Since the "success" of deterrence shows itself in the *absence* of events (namely, an attack or a full-scale war), the interpretation of what significance may be attached to that absence is the key to whether one believes in deterrence or not.

39. See Robert Griffith, *The Politics of Fear* (Lexington: University Press of Kentucky, 1970); Michael Rogin, *The Intellectuals and McCarthy: The Radical Specter* (Cambridge, Mass.: MIT Press, 1967).

40. The literature on the MX/Peacekeeper missile is exceptionally large. A sampling of writings in sources concentrating on military matters includes the following: Edgar Ulsamer, "U.S. Strategic Deterrence at the Crossroads," *Air Force Magazine* 60 (December 1977): 42-49; "The $100 Million Mobile Missile; The MX and the Future of U.S. Strategic Forces," *Defense Monitor* 6 (August 1977), entire issue; "MX Impact to Be Limited," *Air Force Times* 38 (13 February 1978), 35; Lt Gen Thomas P. Stafford, "The Challenge of M-X," *Signal* 34 (September 1979): 8-12; Norman Polmar, "The Infinite Silo," *Sea Power* 22 (March 1979): 17-21; G. K. Burke, "The MX and Strategic Deterrence in the 1980s," *Air University Review* 30 (May-June 1979): 28-38; Edward A. Miller, Jr., "The MX and the Environment," *Air Force Policy Letter for Commanders*, supplement no. 12 (December 1979): 8-12; Harry F. Eustace, "MX Fiasco: Will It Legislate a New Market?" *Electronic Warfare/Defense Electronics* 11 (April 1979): 33; Colin S. Gray, "The MX ICBM: Why We Need It," *Air Force Magazine* 62 (August 1979): 66-68; "MX Missile Basing Plans Detailed," *International Defense Review* 12, no. 8, 1284-85; Lt Gen Ira C. Eaker "The MX Missile Decision," *Air Force Times* 39 (9 July 1979): 13-14; "MX Missile Mobile Basing System," *Interavia* 34 (November 1979): 1006-8; Len Famiglietti, "MX Mobile Concept: 50,000 People," *Air Force Times* 39 (5 March 1979): 4; Lawrence J. Korb, "The Case for the MX," *Air University Review* 31 (July-August 1980): 2-10; Donald M. Snow, "The MX-Basing Mode Muddle—Issues and Alternatives," *Air University Review* 31 (July-August 1980): 11-25; Senator E. J. Garn, "SUM (Shallow Underwater Missile): It Doesn't Add Up," *Armed Forces Journal International* 117 (January 1980): 36-37; Senator Mark O. Hatfield, "SUM (Shallow Underwater Missile) Strategy," *Armed Forces Journal International* 117 (January 1980): 35-36; Merle MacBain, "SUM (Shallow Underwater Mobile): The Bottom Line—A Coastal Alternative to the Great Wall Concept," *Sea Power* 22 (December 1979): 42-44; "Solar Power for MX?" *Armed Forces Journal International* 117 (January 1980): 8; Lt Gen Ira C. Eaker, "Will the MX Missile Survive?" *Air Force Times* 40 (24 March 1980): 13-14; Lt Gen Kelly H. Burke, "Why the U.S. Must Have the MX Missile," *Air Reservist* 32 (May 1980): 3; Blair Stewart, "MX and the Counterforce Problem: A Case for Silo Deployment," *Strategic Review* 9 (Summer 1981): 16-26; Bernard T. Feld and Kosta Tsipis, "Land-based Intercontinental Ballistic Missiles," *Asian Defense Journal* 9 (September 1981): 19-21; "Major Alternate MX Basing Concepts," *Defense Electronics* 13 (November 1981): 78-79; John Ginovsky, "Southwest MX System Will Disturb Environment," *Air Force Times* 41 (2 February 1981): 12; Leonard Famiglietti, "Titan Silos to House MXs: Shell Game

Scrapped," *Air Force Times* 42 (12 October 1981): 4; Adam M. Garfinkle, "Dense Pack: A Critique and An Alternative," *Parameters* 12 (December 1982): 14-23; Edgar Ulsamer, "For MX: Closely Spaced Basing," *Air Force Magazine* 65 (November 1982): 20. Among other works, also see a steady series of articles in *Aviation Week* in 1977 and after, such as J. M. Lenorovitz, "Air Force Restudying Basing Plan," *Aviation Week* 110 (15 January 1979): 21; P. J. Klauss, "MX Basing Studies Show Vertical Silo Preference," *Aviation Week* 108 (19 June 1978): 22-23. Also see Colin S. Gray, "Strategic Forces Triad: End of the Road?" *Foreign Affairs* 56 (July 1978): 771-89; "Missile X: Carter Will Get Two Choices," *Business Week*, 25 December 1978, 36; "MX: Carter Woos the Senate," *U.S. News and World Report* 86 (18 June 1979): 4; Morton Kondracke, "Trench Warfare: MX Missile," *The New Republic* 180 (16 June 1979): 13-15; W. H. Kincade, "Will MX Backfire?" *Foreign Policy* 37 (Winter 1979): 43-58.

41. The urgency of the matter for President Carter was suggested by his commitment to the deployment scheme popularly termed "racetrack" which, with its very large requirements of land, water, and other resources, was regarded as an ecological problem of the first order by the very groups with whom President Carter had been closely associated in various other environment-related issues throughout his administration. For a president, generally regarded by environmentally conscious groups as among the most effective and enlightened public officials, to adopt a plan for MX deployment that was about the worst those same groups could envision, suggests the measure of President Carter's concern on the matter of the Triad. See E. R. Ricciuti, "Salting the Desert with ICBMs," *Audubon* 81 (November 1979): 162.

42. On the matter of basing the MX, works include "MX Missile Basing Plans Detailed," *International Defense Review* 12, no. 8 (July-August 1980); "MX Missile Mobile Basing System," *Interavia* 34 (November 1979); "The MX-Basing Mode Muddle," *Air University Review* (July-August 1980); "SUM (Shallow Underwater Missile) Strategy," *Armed Forces Journal International* 117 (January 1980); "Major Alternate MX Basing Concepts," *Defense Electronics* 13 (November 1981); and "Dense Pack: A Critique and An Alternative," *Parameters* 12 (December 1982).

43. This plan, called Deep Underground Missile Basing, surely yielded the most infelicitous acronym since MAD.

44. Homer Lea, *The Valor of Ignorance* (New York: Macmillan, 1909).

45. The study, conducted by James Gerr, Gerald Davison, and Robert Gatchel, is described in Maggie Scarf, *Body, Mind, Behavior* (Washington, D.C.: The New Republic Book Co., 1976).

46. The deterioration of French, Chinese, and British strength after World War II created a sense of urgency and obligation to new world duties among many in the United States; and, in a world with just two major active power centers at the time, it was altogether too easy to confuse accepting worldwide commitments with actually having one's way. The reemergence of a far more diverse world restored a more natural interaction in the world, characterized by influence rather than control; but, for those whose own experience was with the more eccentric phenomenon of control, the adjustment itself may easily have been taken as eccentric and abnormal.

APPENDIX A

DEPARTMENT OF THE AIR FORCE
AIR UNIVERSITY
CENTER FOR AEROSPACE DOCTRINE, RESEARCH, AND EDUCATION
MAXWELL AIR FORCE BASE, AL 36112-5532

Captain Marty Dupont   26 March 1984
SAF/LLI
Pentagon
Washington DC 20330

Dear Captain Dupont

Enclosed is a copy of the letter which is being sent today to Congressional offices, consistent with our brief conversation over the telephone. As we had agreed, I would provide additional background information concerning my current research project at CADRE to serve as explanatory material for those Congressional offices which might want it. I have also sought to use the opportunity to express thanks to those who have already responded (about 100 offices as now). As you'll see, I have specifically noted that this new letter does not entail any additional request. This letter, like the first one, has been sent to the offices of all Senators and Congressmen.

Good wishes.

Sincerely,

DONALD J. MROZEK   1 Atch
Visiting Research Fellow   Letter to Members of Congress
Airpower Research Institute

DEPARTMENT OF THE AIR FORCE
AIR UNIVERSITY
CENTER FOR AEROSPACE DOCTRINE, RESEARCH, AND EDUCATION
MAXWELL AIR FORCE BASE, AL 36112-5532

I would appreciate your sending what you would consider your representative statements of views concerning US policy toward El Salvador, Nicaragua, and Lebanon.

Thank you for your assistance.

Sincerely,

DONALD J. MROZEK
Visiting Research Fellow
Airpower Research Institute

APPENDIX B

Questions Posed of the Data, 1980

1. Respondent's name

2. Affiliation: Senate or House

3. State represented

4. Party affiliation: Democrat or Republican

5. Sex: Male or female

6. Are there references to the US experience in Vietnam?

7. Is there evidence of support for current administration policy in the Middle East?

8. Is there evidence of support for current administration policy in Central America?

9. Is there evidence of support for current administration policy toward Nicaragua?

10. Is there evidence of support for current administration policy toward El Salvador?

11. Is there evidence of support for current administration policy toward Lebanon?

12. Is the USSR or Cuba mentioned as a possible or probable source of troubles in El Salvador and Central America?

13. Is a lack of strategic clarity identified as a problem in US policy toward Lebanon?

14. Is a lack of strategic clarity identified as a problem in US policy toward Central America?

15. Is a lack of strategic clarity identified as a problem in US policy in, and action during, the Vietnam War?

16. Is the prospect of large migrations of refugees from Latin America mentioned as a present danger?

17. Is US security claimed to be at stake and at risk in Lebanon?

18. Is US security claimed to be at stake and at risk in Central America?

19. Is a failure to match tactical means and strategic ends said to be at the heart of US troubles in regional unrest and conflict?

20. Is there mention of possible worth in invoking the War Powers Act?

INDEX

A

Afghanistan: 95–96
Air Force doctrine: 7–8, 17
Air Force Magazine: 20
AirLand Battle: 22–23, 25–27, 29, 41–42
Air University Review: x, 43, 45
Allard, Dean C.: 16
American Civil War: 2, 5, 15, 62
Anderson, Jack: 55
Andropov, Yuri: 98

B

Bagley, Worth: 59–60
Ball, George W.: 56
Baltimore Sun: 56, 57, 101
Bay of Pigs: 96
Becker, Carl: 5
Bennett, Charles (congressman): 76
Berkeley, Gerald: 15
Bergson, Henri: 6
Biden, Joseph R., Jr. (senator): 87–88
Bingaman, Jeff (senator): 96
Bishop, Maurice (prime minister, Grenada): 97
"Blanket" explanations of policy: 74, 79–81, 88, 103
Blumenson, Martin: 16
"Boat people": 83–85
Bonker, Don (congressman): 79
Britt, Robin (congressman): 85
Business Week: 97

C

Cardwell, Col Thomas A., III: 26
Carter, Jimmy: 95, 106
Central America: 19–20, 55–57, 60–62, 72, 89, 95–96, 97, 103
Central American Defense Council (Condeca): 55
Central Command (CENTCOM): 28
Cheney, Richard (congressman): 75, 80
Chicago Tribune: 61
Christian Science Monitor: 56

Clausewitz, Carl von: 10, 15, 45, 47
"Cold war consensus": xi, 69, 81ff, 90, 105, 109
Colorado Springs Sun: 21
Congressional Record: 75
Contras: 74, 96
Counterinsurgency: 28, 38, 40–42, 84, 86, 96
Craig, Larry E. (congressman): 85
Cranston, Alan (senator): 81
Crowl, Phillip A.: 46
Cuba: 44, 73, 79, 81–83, 85–87, 96, 97, 109

D

Danforth, John (senator): 96
Denton, Jeremiah (senator): 86
Dick, Lt Gen William W., Jr.: 24
Dickinson, William L. "Bill" (congressman): 83
Doctrine (military in general): 2, 11, 21, 23, 25, 27, 28, 38, 45
Durenberger, David (senator): 77–79

E

Eagleton, Thomas (senator): 76
Eisenhower, Dwight: 29, 75
El Salvador: 10, 28, 55, 57, 60–61, 71–72, 74–75, 78, 79–80, 83, 85, 87–88, 96, 103
Escalation: 12

F

Force structure: 2–3
Ford, Gerald: 58, 84
Franco-Prussian War: 6
Frank, Barney (congressman): 74–75
Futrell, Robert Frank: 16

G

Garment, Suzanne: 59
Gelb, Leslie H.: 59

Gemayel, Bashir: 77
Geyelin, Philip: 44, 57
Gold, Philip: 58
Gonzalez, Henry B. (congressman): 87
Great Britain: 70, 95
Greene, Gen Wallace: 24
Grenada: 57, 95, 97, 99–102
Grunwald, Henry: 102
Guevara, Che: 53
Gulf of Tonkin Resolution: 76

H

Hall, Sam B. (congressman): 76, 85
Hamilton, Alexander: 10
Hansen, James V. (congressman): 84
Hart, Gary (senator): 61–62, 89
Hartnett, Thomas P. (congressman): 84
Henderickson, Paul: 6–7
Herring, George C.: 101–2
Herspring, Dale R.: 44
Ho Chi Minh Trail: 12
Honduras: 61, 83, 87
Hooper, Brickford: 16

I

Indochina monographs: see US Army Center of Military History
Inouye, Daniel K. (senator): 88
Interservice rivalry: 29
Israel: 95

J

Johnson, Lyndon B: 11, 12, 97

K

Kelley, Gen Paul X.: 99
Kennedy administration: 11, 54
Kindness, Thomas N. (congressman): 83
Kissinger commission: 75
Koch, Edward (mayor, New York City): 63
Korean War: 9–10, 38, 57
Krepinevich, Andrew F., Jr.: 27–28

L

Lagomarsino, Robert J. (congressman): 84–85
Lea, Homer: 107
Lebanon: 10, 21, 56–57, 59, 61–62, 71, 74, 76–77, 86–87, 95, 98–100
Lehman, John (secy navy): 98
Lehman, Richard H. (congressman): 80
Low-intensity conflict: 38, 41–42, 44

M

Machos, Maj James A.: 25–26
Madison, James: 10
Mahan, Alfred Thayer: 45–46, 47
Mao: 96
Marine Corps Gazette: 28
Marks, Edward: 3
Mayaguez incident: 58
McCain, John (congressman): 77
McConnell, Gen John P.: 24–25
McFarlane, Robert: 77
McNamara, Robert S. (secy defense): 6–7, 17
Media relations: 18, 42
Mexico: 20, 70, 83
Meyer, Gen Edward C.: 19
Middleton, Drew: 18–19, 96
Military organization: 5
Military Review: 25–26
Milton, Gen T. R.: 20–21
Mitchell, George (senator): 79–80
Mohr, Charles: 62
Momyer, William W.: 16–17
Mondale, Walter: 61, 62

N

National Journal: 26
National Security Council (NSC): 11
National War College: 3
Naval War College: 46–48
Naval War College Review: 43–46
Nelson, Bill (congressman): 75, 80
Newsweek: 28
New York Times: 59, 62, 96, 103
Nicaragua: 10, 55, 61, 71–72, 74, 75, 80, 83–85, 96–97
North American Treaty Organization: 19, 23, 39–40
Nutting, Gen Wallace: 19

O

O'Neill, Thomas P. (congressman): 98
Objectives of war and policy: see war aims
Office of Air Force History: 16

P

Palladino, Michael P.: 28–29
Palmer, Gen Dave Richard: 9
Panama Canal: 79, 83, 85
Panetta, Leon (congressman): 88
Parameters: 43
Pastora, Eden: 74
"Peacekeeper" missile (MX): 105–8
Pentagon Papers: 6–7
Porter, Gareth: 44
Principles of war: 8, 10, 15, 45

R

Ray, Richard (congressman): 76
Reagan, Ronald: 56, 59, 60, 61, 62, 76, 77, 97, 98, 102–3, 105–6
Rogers, Gen Bernard: 9, 19
Rosenfeld, Stephen S.: 60
Rostow, Walt W.: 12, 44
Rumsfeld, Donald: 77

S

Safire, William: 98
San Antonio Light: 87
Sanders, Sol: 97
San Diego Union: 55
Schaefer, Dan (congressman): 85
Schweitzer, Lt Gen Robert L.: 19
Sharp, Adm U. S. Grant: 16–17
Shelby, Richard (congressman): 83, 85
Shulimson, Jack: 16
Shultz, George (secy state): 97
Sims, Williams S.: 46
Skelton, Ike (congressman): 77
Slattery, Jim (congressman): 81
Smith, Lawrence J. (congressman): 75
Sonnenfeldt, Helmut: 44
Soviet Union: see Union of Soviet Socialist Republics
Special Operations Command (SOCOM): 28
Special Warfare Center: 27

Starry, Gen Donn A.: 9, 14
Stennis, John (senator): 60
Stockdale, Rear Adm James B.: 44
Stone, Marvin: 55–56
Strategic goals: see war aims
Studds, Gerry E. (congressman): 75, 87
Summers, Col Harry, Jr. (congressman): 10–11, 13–15, 102–3
Survey: 97

T

Tactical Air Command (TAC): 25–26
Taylor, Gen Maxwell D.: 23, 77
Technological innovation: 3, 24
Tet offensive (1968): 13
Thatcher, Margaret: 102
Thucydides: 47
Tonkin Gulf Resolution: see Gulf of Tonkin Resolution
Townsend, Patrick L.: 28–29
TRADOC: see US Army Training and Doctrine Command
Truman, Harry: ix, 29, 76
Turner, Stansfield: 47

U

Union of Soviet Socialist Republics (USSR): 82, 85–87, 95–97, 105
US Army Center of Military History: 8
US Army Command and General Staff College: 37–43
US Army Training and Doctrine Command: 23, 25
US Army War College: 43
USA Today: 60
US Congress: 4, 20, 26, 56–57, 69–90
U.S. News & World Report: 55

V

Vessey, Gen John W., Jr.: 19
Vietnam studies: see US Army Center of Military History
"Vietnam syndrome": 58–59
Vietnam Veterans Memorial: 62–63

W

Wall Street Journal: 59
War aims: 1–2, 58, 82, 89
War of 1812: 62
War Powers Act: 60, 76–77, 86–87
Warsaw Pact: 23, 26–27
Washington Post: 6, 19, 57, 60
Washington Times: 58, 59
Waxman, Henry (congressman): 76
Weinberger, Caspar (secy defense): 59
Westmoreland, Gen William C.: 16, 19
Wicker, Tom: 103
Wickham, Gen John A., Jr.: 19–20
Will, George: 96
Wills, Garry: 56
Wilson, Pete (senator): 84
Wilson, Woodrow: 6
World War I: 6
World War II: 29, 53, 57, 70, 104

Y

Yarborough, Lt Gen William P.: 27–28

Z

Zumwalt, Adm Elmo: 59–60